VAULT GUIDE TO THE
CASE
INTERVIEW

VAULT GUIDE TO THE
CASE INTERVIEW

MARK ASHER, ERIC CHUNG
AND THE STAFF OF VAULT

For information about permission to reproduce selections from this book, contact Vault Inc.,
150 W. 22nd St., 5th Floor, New York, NY 10011, (212) 366-4212.

Library of Congress CIP Data is available.

ISBN 10: 1-58131-530-9

ISBN 13: 978-58131-530-1

Printed in the United States of America

ACKNOWLEDGMENTS

Vault's acknowledgments: We are extremely grateful to Vault's entire staff for all their help in the editorial, production and marketing processes. Vault also would like to acknowledge the support of our investors, clients, employees, family, and friends. Thank you!

Appreciation
Achievement • Being
Belonging • Becoming
Development • Diversity
Enhancement • Enjoyment
Positive • Experiences • People
Friends • Family • Flexibility
Freedom • Fullfillment • Happiness
Health • Hopes • Identity
Improvement • Integrity
Knowledge • Nurture
Opportunities • Opinions
Satisfaction • Security
Truth • Dreams

Quality of Life

What is your definition of QUALITY of life? At Gallup, you'll work in a culture that SUPPORTS you not just professionally, but personally. Whether your PASSION is building new business, managing consulting projects, or assisting executives, you'll have the OPPORTUNITY to do what you do BEST every day. We'll help you discover your TALENTS and build STRENGTHS.

How do we know that life is BETTER at Gallup? **A recent survey by Vault.com of 2,500 consultants ranks Gallup #1 for corporate culture and work-life balance, and as #2 for overall quality of life.**

At Gallup, we offer more than just a job — we offer you a FUTURE.

www.gallup.com/careers/

Table of Contents

BEING THERE   59

REAL LIFE INTERVIEWS   67

BUSINESS CASES   73

INTERACTIVE CASES   111

PRESENTATION CASES   137

GUESSTIMATES   193

BRAINTEASERS   209

Visit the Vault Consulting Career Channel at www.vault.com/consulting — with
insider firm profiles, message boards, the Vault Finance Job Board and more.

VAULT CAREER LIBRARY   xiii

FINAL ANALYSIS   219

APPENDIX   223

Introduction

Why the Case?

Your impressive resume may get you an interview with a consulting firm, but it won't get you the job. Consultants know that a resume, at its very best, is only a two-dimensional representation of a multi-faceted, dynamic person.

And because consulting firms depend on employing those multi-faceted, dynamic people, the firms rely heavily on the case interview to screen candidates. The interview process is especially pertinent in the consulting industry, since consulting professionals spend the lion's share of their business day interacting with clients and colleagues and must themselves constantly interview client employees and executives.

Consultants must have a select set of personality and leadership traits in order to be successful. The consultant's work environment is extremely turbulent. There are nonstop co-worker changes, hostile client environments, countless political machinations, and near-perpetual travel. These factors mandate that an individual be cool under pressure, be influential without being condescending, be highly analytical, have the ability to understand the smallest aspects of a problem (while simultaneously seeing the big picture), and have the ability to maintain a balance between the personal and professional.

Consultants are often staffed in small groups in far-flung areas. As a result, the individual must be able to function, and function well, without many of the traditional workplace standards: a permanent working space, the ability to return home each night, easily accessed services such as administrative assistance, faxing, and photocopying, and the camaraderie that develops among co-workers assigned to the same business unit.

All these factors necessitate a unique interview structure focused on assessing a candidate's ability to manage these particular circumstances with professionalism and excellence. The case interview has evolved as a method for evaluating these characteristics.

Visit the Vault Consulting Career Channel at **www.vault.com/consulting** — with insider firm profiles, message boards, the Vault Consulting Job Board and more.

VAULT CAREER LIBRARY

1

What is a Case?

Simply put, a case interview is the analysis of a business question. Unlike most other interview questions, it is an interactive process. Your interviewer will present you with a business problem and ask you for your opinion. Your job is to ask the interviewer logical questions that will permit you to make a detailed recommendation. The majority of case interviewers don't have a specific answer that you, the candidate, are expected to give. What the interviewer is looking for is a thought process that is both analytical and creative (what consultants love to call "out-of-the-box" thinking). Specific knowledge of the industry covered by the case question is a bonus but not necessary. Business school students and candidates with significant business world experience receive case questions that require a deeper understanding of business models and processes.

The interview with a consulting company normally lasts about half an hour. Of this time, about 5 to 10 minutes is taken up with preliminary chat and behavioral questions and five minutes of you asking questions about the company. This leaves 5 to 15 minutes for your case interview question or questions. Make them count!

Types of Case Interviews

What case interviews are not designed to do is to explore educational, professional, or experiential qualifications. If you've reached the case interview stage, take a deep breath – the consulting firm has already weighed your background, GPA, and experience and found you worthy of a deeper skill assessment. This means that the case interview is yours to lose. Triumph over your case interviews and chances are that a slot at the firm will open for you.

Case interviews vary widely, but in general they fall into three groups: business cases, guesstimates, and brainteasers.

Case interviews

Case interviews vary somewhat in their format. The classic and most common type of case interview is the business case, in which you're presented with a business scenario and asked to analyze it and make recommendations. Most cases are presented in oral form, though some involve handouts or slides, and a few (like Monitor Company's) are entirely written. (In a written case, the interviewer will not contribute any other information besides what's on the handout.) Another variation on the case interview is the group case interview, where three to six candidates are grouped together and told to solve a case cooperatively. Consultants from the firm watch as silent observers. Some firms now ask candidates to do presentations. Though you should certainly be prepared for these variations on case interviews, you are most likely to come across the traditional, *mano-a-mano* case interview.

Guesstimates

Whether free-standing or as part of a case, learning how to make "back-of-the-envelope" calculations (rough, yet basically accurate) is an essential part of the case interview. As part of a guesstimate, you might be asked to estimate how many watermelons are sold in the United States each year, or what the market size for a new computer program that organizes your wardrobe might be. (For example, you might need to figure out the market size for the wardrobe software as a first step in determining how to enter the European market.) You will not be expected to get the exact number, but you should come close – hence the guesstimate. Non-business school students and others who appear to be weak quantitatively may get stand-alone guesstimates – guesstimates given independently of a case.

Brainteasers

Brainteasers are normally logic puzzles or riddles. They may be timed. Often, brainteasers are meant to test both analytic and "out-of-the-box" thinking, as well as grace under pressure.

Skills Assessed in the Case Interview

Following your case interview, your consulting interviewer will complete a written evaluation form. The evaluation forms often include a list of qualities, traits, and abilities and ask the interviewer to assess the candidate against the list. Following is a list of these special traits that, according to consulting insiders, interviewers will be keeping an eye out for as you work through the case interview:

Visit the Vault Consulting Career Channel at **www.vault.com/consulting** — with
insider firm profiles, message boards, the Vault Consulting Job Board and more.

V/\ULT CAREER LIBRARY

3

Leadership skills

You'll hear this from every consulting firm out there – they want leaders. Why, you might ask, would a consulting firm need a leader? After all, many beginning consultants are consigned to number-crunching and research. The fact is, however, that consultants are often called upon to work independently, shape projects with very little direction, and direct others. You should demonstrate your leadership skills by taking charge of the case interview. Ask your questions confidently. Inquire whether the case interview relates to the interviewer's own experience. While your resume and previous leadership experience will probably most strongly convey your leadership ability, your demeanor in the case interview can help.

Analytical skills

The core competency of consulting is analysis – breaking down data, formulating it into a pattern that makes sense, and deriving a sensible conclusion or recommendation. You should display this skill through your efficient, on-target, and accurate questions while wrestling your case to a solution.

Presentation skills

Presenting your analysis is an essential part of consulting. Once consultants have analyzed their case engagement and decided on the proper course of action, they must present their findings and recommendations to their case team and to their clients. Interviewers will be watching you closely to see if you stumble over words, use inadvisable fillers like "um" or "like" frequently, or appear jittery under close questioning. Remember: When you're speaking, slow down and smile. If asked a question that temporarily stumps you, take a deep breath and pause. It's always better to pause than babble. Ask the interviewer to restate information if necessary.

Energy

Even the most qualified and analytical consultant won't be much good if she quits at 5 p.m. during a long and arduous engagement. Interviewers look for zest and energy – firm handshake, sincere and warm smile, bright eyes. Remember that consulting firms expect you to take a long flight and show up at work the next day alert, perky, and ready to go. If you must, drink lots of coffee and use eyedrops – just be energized.

Attention to detail/Organization

Consultants must be as painstaking as scientists in their attention to detail. And consultants who juggle two or more flights a week and engagements all over the world must be extremely organized. You can display this skill through a disciplined, logical approach to your case solution, and by showing up for your interview prepared. You'll want to take notes, so bring a pad of paper and a pen. Interviewers notice when candidates must ask for these materials. You must arrive on time.

Quantitative skills

Those spreadsheets you'll be working with as a management consultant need numbers to fill them. Consulting interviews will inevitably test your grasp of numbers and your ability to manipulate them. Many interviewers will assess your quantitative skills by giving you a "guesstimate," either within the case question or separately.

Flexibility

Consultants may have to arrive at the office one day and be packed off to Winnipeg for six months the next. This kind of flexibility of schedule is mirrored in tests for mental flexibility. To test your grasp of a case interview, the interviewer may suddenly introduce a new piece of information ("Okay, let's say the factories must be opened either in Canada or China") or flip the terms of the case interview ("What if this labor contract is not guaranteed, as I said earlier?") and then watch how quickly you're able to alter your thinking.

Maturity

Consultants must often work with executives and company officials decades older than they are. (This is why consultants are taught the right way to answer the question, "How old are you?") Eliminate giggling, fidgeting, and references to awesome fraternity events you may have attended, even if the interviewer seems receptive.

Intelligence, a.k.a. "mental horsepower"

Rather straightforward – consulting interviewers are looking for quickness of analysis and depth of insight. Don't be afraid to ask questions for fear of looking stupid – smart people learn by asking questions and assimilating new information. At the same time, asking your interviewer to repeat an elementary (or irrelevant) concept 20 times will not do you any favors.

What Kind of Case Will I Get?

While there's no way to tell for sure what case question you'll get, there are some things that can tip you off to the kind of case you'll receive.

If you're an undergraduate or other non-MBA student, you can probably be safely assured of getting a creative or "open-ended" question. "We don't expect our undergraduate candidates to know that much about business," confides one interviewer. "What we do expect is the ability to break down and articulate complex concepts." Undergraduates are also much more likely to get guesstimates and brainteasers than MBAs.

Are you a business school student or graduate? Then your case question will probably be less open-ended and drive toward an actual solution. Your interviewer may posit something from her own experience – knowing what course of action the consultancy actually ended up recommending. This doesn't mean you have to make the same recommendation – but you'd better be able to back up your reasoning! Alternatively, one thing case interviewers love to do is look at your resume and give you a case question that relates to your past experience. "For example," says one consultant, "if you were on the advertising staff for the school newspaper, you might be given a question about investing in advertising agencies." For this reason, advise consultants, "it makes sense to follow up on your field in *The Wall Street Journal* because you may be asked about recent developments in it. If you know what's going on you'll be that much more impressive." Some guesstimates, like figuring out the total worldwide revenues of *Shrek 2*, are broad enough so that most people can make a reasonable assumption of numbers.

CASE
STRATEGIES

Your Objective

Business cases involve real-world situations for which a candidate is provided with a set of facts about a business or business problem. Business cases can be presented as a narrative detailed by the interviewer (most common) or on paper. They may also take the form of a case study, where the candidate is presented with a packet of text including graphs, charts, financial information, and other exhibits.

Regardless of the format, the objective of the business case remains the same. The interviewer is attempting to assess your ability to synthesize many different situational elements into a cohesive understanding of the problem at hand. As a candidate, you will need to draw upon your analytical abilities, business experience, and deductive reasoning to crack the case. In most cases, the business case will be timed, and can last anywhere from 15 minutes to an hour. (While you will usually be given only one case in an interview, you may be given two or more shorter cases.)

In some situations, business cases may be presented with little or no information. The interviewer may simply toss out a few facts like, "We have a multi-billion dollar consumer products client with operations in 15 countries. What would you advise them?" Then the interviewer falls silent. In addition to appraising the aforementioned skills, the interviewer may deliberately choose this vagueness to assess a candidate's poise, reaction to an unfamiliar situation, overall confidence, and grace under pressure.

Don't Fret!

There are no "correct" answers to business case questions. In fact, many times you will not reach a conclusion before the interviewer moves on to other questions. This is not a sign that something has gone terribly wrong. The interviewer is not looking for a definitive answer. Rather he is assessing your ability to analyze and synthesize various facts, clarify the situation, and set up a framework for pursuing other information. If you have already successfully demonstrated that you have the capability to perform these tasks, your interviewer may wish to move on to a different subject or case. In fact, if the interviewer moves on to another case, it shows that you're still a viable candidate. "If you've screwed up," states an interviewer, "they'll probably just spend the rest of the time on chit chat."

Top 10 tips for answering business case questions successfully

1. Take notes

As your interviewer presents your case, be sure to take careful notes on the numbers or other facts given. (Always bring a notepad and a pen to a consulting interview.) If you plan on drawing graphs, add brownie points by bringing graph paper (which shows major foresight). Take notes so you don't have to ask your interviewer to repeat information.

2. Make no assumptions

As a case interviewee, you should never make any assumptions. Your interviewer will inevitably leave things out of the case presented to you. (If an apple juice manufacturer has seen its expenses rise dramatically, for example, your interviewer probably won't mention the tree blight that's constricting the supply of apples.) You should assume the persona of an actual consultant trying to learn about an assignment. You should also ask if the company has encountered a similar problem, or what other companies in the field have done when faced with similar situations. Your interviewer may not release that information but will be impressed that you asked these sensible questions. Some good basic "professional" questions to ask, which apply to most cases:

• What is the product?

• Who hired us?

• How long will this engagement last?

• Has the company faced this problem (or opportunity) before? If so, how did it react? What was the outcome?

• What have other companies facing this situation done?

3. Ask questions

Your interviewer expects you to ask questions – as many intelligent questions as you need to obtain an accurate picture of the relevant facts in the case. Many inexperienced case interviewees make the error of asking their interviewer too few questions. They may be afraid that they will look ignorant, or not wish to "bother" the interviewer. Remember – not asking questions is a fatal error in a case interview. If you don't know the first thing about the helicopter market, ask how much it costs to manufacture a rotor. If you need to estimate the demand for a beef-flavored potato snack in Wichita, Kansas, then feel free to ask the population of Wichita and environs.

You will often find that your interviewer will direct your line of questioning to a specific area, but you must always be ready to control the conversation in case the interviewer does not direct your reasoning. If you are unsure, simply ask the interviewer. For instance, if you find the interviewer offering little direction as you move through your initial questions, you may wish to ask, "I find the lack of a risk assessment to be a potential showstopper. Might I ask some detailed questions about this?" Or you might say, "Given what you have told me about the situation, I would like to find out more about the client's current relationship with its distribution partner. Would that be OK?" In this way, you take charge of the line of questioning without stepping on the interviewer's role.

4. Listen to the answers you get

One interviewer warns: "Many candidates get so caught up in asking the perfect questions that they don't listen to the answers they receive. They go through a mental list of all the questions they want to ask, and ignore the response they got. That throws off their reasoning." Make sure you respond to the information you receive and incorporate it into your analysis.

5. Maintain eye contact

Always maintain direct eye contact during the case interview. Eye contact is critical when answering case questions – it demonstrates confidence and authority. Remember that in consulting you may find yourself in front of 20 executives at a major corporation presenting a strategy you were briefed on only a half-hour ago. And then you have to answer questions! So you can see why business case interviewing is so important to consulting – it simulates the work environment consultants must face every day.

6. Take your time

It's perfectly fine to take a minute to think through your answer – in fact, most interviewers find it preferable. "Whenever I asked to take the time out to collect my thoughts," reports one consultant who's undergone "dozens" of case interviews, "my interviewers always said, 'Okay, good, go ahead.'" On the other hand, while "a minute of deep thinking" is fine, "five minutes is really overkill. You don't want your interviewer waiting there for five minutes. The case is only supposed to be 15 or 20 minutes."

7. Lay out a road map for your interviewer

After you've selected your approach, don't keep it a secret. Tell your interviewer what approach you're going to take. For example, you might say, "First, I'm going to discuss the Mexican and Canadian markets. Second, I'll ask about our entry strategy. Finally, I'm making a recommendation." "One of the most important things consultants have to do is present complex ideas in a lucid manner," explains one interviewer. "That's why you should take time to explain your reasoning. Not only will it impress your interviewer and allow you to confirm any assumption that you're making, but it will allow you to get your own thinking straight."

8. Think out loud

In order to navigate case interviews successfully, you will need to act quickly and confidently. The business case is an opportunity to show the interviewer how you think. Your interviewer wants to know that you can reason in a rapid and logical fashion. As you assess, compile, and analyze the elements presented to you, be sure that you speak aloud and explain your reasoning. This is the only way the interviewer can assess your performance.

You may not be entirely comfortable thinking out loud. So if you're not feeling confident thinking aloud, try practicing by yourself. Start with something simple like explaining aloud to yourself how to change a tire or how you brush your teeth. Minimize "ums" and other fillers, so that what you say is concise, direct and clear.

Next, try practicing on friends or family. Have them ask questions for which you must assess a situation. For example, they might ask, "I'm not sure at which bank I should open a checking account. What are the trade-offs between Bank X and Bank Y?" or "I've got $50 to spend on groceries, so what should I buy?" Even speaking to yourself in front of the mirror will build your confidence thinking "on the fly" while simultaneously speaking.

9. Present your thinking in a clear, logical manner. Where useful, use frameworks and business concepts to organize your answer

You should develop a framework for assessing case interview questions which can be applied to different situations. In general, in any situation you will want to:

• Understand the scope of the engagement

• Pinpoint the objectives

• Identify the key players

• Work towards a recommendation

Beyond this, you may choose any line of questioning or structure with which you feel comfortable. As you practice, you will find yourself developing this framework unconsciously as you attempt to gain clarity over a situation. Capture and package this framework, and have it available by memory (or on paper if you wish) for use at any time.

Where useful, also use advanced business concepts and frameworks – such as Porter's Five Forces or Value Chain Analysis – (see the chapter on case frameworks) to help organize your thoughts and impress your interviewer.

10. Quickly summarize your conclusions

You have limited time in your case interview to make your point. If you are uncomfortable with quickly summarizing your conclusions, think about being faced with this classic situation:

"A consultant working for a multinational corporation inadvertently bumped into the CEO of the corporation while waiting for the elevator. As they got on the elevator, the CEO announced that he was on his way to a Board of Directors meeting on the 34th floor. He then instructed the consultant to brief him completely on the major findings of the project in the time it took the elevator to go from the 1st floor to the 34th floor."

While this is no doubt an urban legend, it is extremely likely that you will encounter time-pressured situations many times in your professional career, especially in consulting, where time is a precious commodity. If you are taking a while reaching your conclusion, your interviewer may ask you for the "60 second pitch." Practice summarizing your answer in a minute or less.

What if I Get One of Those Group Case Interviews?

While Monitor used to be one of a very few consulting companies that gave a group case interview, its popularity is increasing. In a group interview, between two and five candidates are given a case and asked to present their findings in one hour. A few consultants from the firm remain with the candidates to silently observe their progress.

One important thing to remember is that the group interview is not a zero sum game. "Everyone may get an offer, or no one may get an offer," confirms one consultant. The key with group case interviews is to show your keen organizational and teamwork abilities. Don't bully your fellow candidates, but don't sit back and quietly do as you are told. One recent group case interviewee suggests, "Present your thoughts on how to divide the analysis. Listen to what others have to say. Try to determine areas of expertise. If you disagree with their thoughts or estimates, say so, but never be denigrating or rude. Look like you're having a good time. Otherwise, the analysis is pretty similar to a regular case."

Common Problems and Troubleshooting

Even though the case interview isn't designed to stress you out (brainteasers are another story), invariably, consulting candidates get nervous during their interviews. "Even MBAs get nervous," says one business school student. "You're really on the spot, and you keep thinking about the job."

But, say recent interviewees, don't be so stressed that you assume that you're doomed. "A lot of times, you'll make a recommendation, and the interviewer will start arguing for another outcome. They are just doing that to see if you stick to your guns." On the other hand, if you've done an analysis based on an assumption that is blatantly wrong, and the interviewer makes this point to you – "Well, don't you think your estimation of the annual consumption of electric blankets in the United States as 3 billion is a bit high, considering there are only 275 million people in the country?" – don't blindly stick to a flawed conclusion.

In fact, it's pretty normal to make erroneous assumptions or conclusions during the case interview. One consultant says: "One of the most common mistakes case interviewees make is to screw up once and then freeze. They assume that they've irrevocably ruined their chances at the firm. But in fact, learning from mistakes is a big part of being a consultant. The interviewer will be impressed if the candidate can rebound." "If you go the wrong way, it doesn't necessarily result in a ding," confirms another consultant. "Most interviewers will try to lead you back to the true path. If you can pick up on this and follow their lead, you will still be in the running."

Thinking About the Case

All business case questions ask you to display reasoning or logical thought process. Here are some types of business case questioning with which you should become familiar. While not exhaustive, many business case questions fall into these general categories of thought process:

• **Weigh the pros and cons** – You will be asked to identify and describe the various trade-offs between two or more choices.

• **Break down a complex system** – Given a large multi-faceted problem, sort the problem's pieces into distinct elements and articulate the overall nature of the issue.

• **Resolve a conflict** – When presented with a situation in which two or more elements are in direct dispute or opposition, you will be asked to develop a framework for resolution. There may be no "correct" answer; you must argue successfully for your conclusion.

• **Interpret the numbers** – You will be presented with a series of financial or other quantitative exhibits and be asked to develop and articulate a synthesis of this information, which may involve some basic conclusions (but not necessarily an answer to the problem).

• **Fill in the blanks** – The interviewer will provide you with minimal information. You will be expected to scope the situation through a dialogue with the interviewer and then most probably address one of the other categories listed above.

The Case Checklist

You may be able to tell the difference between the Four Cs and the Four Ps, but don't get so hung up on memorizing frameworks that you forget some basic steps that can make the difference between a great case and one that goes less than smoothly.

Before the case

- **Arrive on time.** Time is money for consultants. If you keep your interviewer waiting, will you also keep clients waiting as well?

- **Take time to assess your surroundings.** Remember, interviews aren't a one-way process. If you're uncomfortable in the office, that's not a good sign.

- **Dress appropriately.** It bears repeating that even though most consulting firms have gone business casual, you should still wear a suit for your interview.

- **Bring the following items with you:** a pen, a watch, a pencil, a pad of paper, some graph paper and a calculator. You may not be allowed to use the calculator, but if you are, you'll be glad you brought one.

During the case

- **Don't ignore the chitchat.** Your interviewer is evaluating you on your potential for poise and teamwork as well as sheer mental horsepower.

- **Be consistent, but not monotonous.** In most consulting firms, interviewers keep notes on what they talked to you about, what you talked about, and your strengths and weaknesses. If you have one joke that you like to tell or one story about your great leadership ability, it'll wear a little thin (in the eyes of your interviewers). At the same time, your interviewers will note inconsistencies in statements that you make.

- **Take notes when your interviewer is describing the case.** Otherwise, you may miss important points.

- **Repeat the case back.** This will both concentrate your mind and let you know if you've conceptualized the case correctly.

- **Don't be afraid to ask for help.** Phrase your questions in the form of a statement (just think — the opposite of *Jeopardy*.) If you're having trouble interpreting a graph, say "I would interpret these numbers as stating that the cost of our production of widgets is rising rapidly. Am I on the right track here?") Your interviewer will be more likely to help you than if you stare at her blankly and plead for mercy.

- **If you screw up, don't panic.** "You can mess up an interview and still get the job," advises one consultant. Remain calm — and ask for pointers on where you went wrong. Consultants like people who ask questions.

After the case

- **Send thank you notes** — the sooner the better. E-mail works, and you will achieve the best results if you cite specific things about the interview.

- **Watch your mouth!** Never discuss a case while you're still in the office — wait until you're at home with friends. If you're taken out to lunch or are sitting in the lobby of the firm, you're still on an interview. Some firms even ask their alumni for assessments of candidates — so that ex-McKinsey consultant next to you in your class may be asked to assess you.

Specific Types of Business Cases

Many business cases can be categorized as one of the following eight common types of business cases. Some cases may be combinations of two or three case types, or require you to solve problems that fall into different categories.

Falling Profits Case

- **In a nutshell:** This type of case asks you to explore the possible reasons behind a company's drop in profits.

- **What this type of question is designed to assess:** Analytical ability, drilldown from a high-level statement, understanding of financial instruments, communication, industry knowledge

- **Useful concepts/frameworks:** Market assessment, BCG matrix, product mix assessment

Some examples of falling profits cases:

> Bunny New Media is an Internet content provider that has had three straight quarters of high profit gains, followed by a 50% drop in profits this quarter. What has happened?

> Hill Construction has been under contract with the City of Los Angeles to build a new subway station. However, Hill's latest financial statement shows a steep decline in profits relative to this time last year. What is the cause of this decline?

New product introduction

- **In a nutshell:** This type of case asks you to recommend a strategy for introducing a new product.

- **What this type of question is designed to assess:** Analytical ability, understanding of brand management, supply chain, communication, industry knowledge

- **Useful concepts/frameworks:** Four Ps, market analysis, competitor analysis, product portfolio assessment

Some examples of new profit product introduction:

> Joe's Aircraft Engines has a new design ready for market. How should they bring it to market?

> Microvilla Software has a new software application they would like to market over the Internet. What do you think?

Entering a new market

- **In a nutshell:** This type of case asks you to analyze whether a company should enter a new market or develop a new line of products or services. (Usually, the new products or services are somehow related to the company's current business.)

- **What this type of question is designed to assess:** Analytical ability, understanding of market dynamics, supply chain dynamics, communication, industry knowledge

- **Useful concepts/frameworks:** Market assessment, product portfolio analysis

Some examples of new market questions:

Hasma Systems, Inc. currently assembles laser printers for several major high-tech companies. One of these companies has approached Hasma about manufacturing calculators. Hasma asked you to provide an analysis of their ability to provide this service. How would you go about your analysis?

A major consumer products manufacturer currently makes soap, detergent, and canned meat products. Most of the company's product portfolio is considered mature, and it has identified two companies for acquisition: one makes frozen juice concentrate, the other makes hair care products. How would you decide which acquisition, if either, is best for the company?

Entering a new geographic market

• **In a nutshell:** This type of case asks you to analyze whether a company should expand into a new country or region.

• **What this type of question is designed to assess:** Analytical ability, understanding of global market dynamics, geographic currency issues, supply chain dynamics, communication, industry knowledge

• **Useful concepts/frameworks:** Market assessment, supply chain analysis, competitor analysis

Some examples of new geographic market questions:

Miller's Wheat Bran wants to introduce its line of bran products in India. How would they go about assessing the feasibility of this idea?

Billy Bo Bob's Chili is the number one cannedchili product in Texas and Oklahoma. The company is interested in introducing their product in California. How would you recommend the company proceed?

Where to locate a new facility ("site selection case")

- **In a nutshell:** The site selection case asks you to evaluate where a company should locate a new plant or other facility (and sometimes, whether the company's entire operations should be relocated).

- **What this type of question is designed to assess:** Analytical ability, understanding of global market dynamics, regulatory environment, import/export environment, supply chain dynamics, communication, industry knowledge

- **Useful concepts/frameworks:** Market assessment, supply chain analysis, competitor analysis

Some examples of site selection cases:

> Yaya Manufacturing assembles bicycles exclusively in the United States. Due to cost pressures, the company is thinking of moving operations to Mexico. What factors would you consider in making this decision?

> A major beverage manufacturer is negotiating with the Indian government to sell its products in India. The government has demanded that the company sell only products made in India, with the added specification that the company open bottling plants in India. What factors should you consider in evaluating this requirement?

Mergers & acquisitions case

- **In a nutshell:** The M&A case asks you to determine whether a particular acquisition would be advisable.

- **What this type of question is designed to assess:** Analytical ability, regulatory environment, supply chain dynamics, communication, industry knowledge

- **Useful concepts/frameworks:** Market assessment, supply chain analysis, competitor analysis, structural analysis

Some examples of M&A cases:

> Club Med is considering the acquisition of a major cruise line. Describe the way you might assess the viability of this decision.

> A software company is interested in acquiring a logistics company to compress their supply chain and reduce their cycle time from manufacturer to retailer. What factors would you consider in determining whether this would be an appropriate decision?

Competitive response case

- **In a nutshell:** A competitive response case asks you to recommend how your client should react to a move by its competitor.

- **What this type of question is designed to assess:** Analytical ability, supply chain dynamics, communication, industry knowledge, market dynamics

- **Useful concepts/frameworks:** Market assessment, supply chain analysis, competitor analysis, structural analysis

More competitive response questions:

> So Pretty Cosmetics sells products only through major department stores. Their major competitor, Porter Cosmetics, has just announced the opening of 10 stand-alone stores. How should So Pretty Cosmetics react?

> Starstruck Video rents and sells video tapes. They have just learned that their competitor, Vader Video, has signed an exclusive deal with Warner Brothers which gives them exclusive rights to offer Warner Brothers videos for 30 days before Starstruck is allowed to offer them. How should Starstruck Video react?

Changes in government/regulatory environment

- **In a nutshell:** This type of case presents a change in the governmental or regulatory environment (for example, a change in the laws of a particular country where a company has operations) and asks you to advise your client.

Visit the Vault Consulting Career Channel at **www.vault.com/consulting** — with
insider firm profiles, message boards, the Vault Consulting Job Board and more.

VAULT CAREER LIBRARY

21

- **What this type of question is designed to assess:** Analytical ability, supply chain dynamics, communication, industry knowledge, market dynamics, regulatory environment

- **Useful concepts/frameworks:** Market assessment, supply chain analysis, competitor analysis, structural analysis, regulatory analysis

Some examples of change in environment questions:

> **La Piñata, Inc. manufactures party supplies in Malaysia. The recent currency upheavals in Asia have caused the Malaysian government to impose heavy tariffs on all exports. What should La Piñata do?**

> **TSC Software is looking to hire 25 software developers from Asia. They are interested in understanding how they might employ these people without asking them to emigrate or importing them as foreign nationals. How would you investigate this?**

CASE
FRAMEWORKS

While you are strongly encouraged to develop your own personal method for understanding and answering case questions, there are some classic models and business concepts that you will find useful in structuring your thinking. "The model and concepts are like a basic recipe," says one consultant. "Any creativity or alteration you make to that model is like seasoning. Your audience – the interviewer – will appreciate it."

We've divided the concepts and frameworks you should know into two levels: basic and advanced. At a minimum, your consulting interviewer will expect you to know the basic concepts and frameworks, even if you have a limited business background. Those with a strong business background (including MBAs) will be expected to have a strong grasp of the advanced concepts as well.

We must remind you that case frameworks are just that – frameworks, not a solution in and of themselves. Don't tell your interviewer "I'm going to use the Four Cs." Just do it!

A special note about the Internet and cases

Consultants are increasingly setting their cases in the past – 1985, 1969, or what have you. The reason is to avoid the use of the Internet as a consideration in business cases.

Basic Concepts and Frameworks

These "starter" concepts are useful touchstones for undergrads and others without significant business experience. They allow you to structure your thinking in the way a consultant's business-minded clients would expect.

Cost-benefit analysis

Case interviews often require you to make a recommendation to a hypothetical consulting client. Cost-benefit analysis is just another way of saying "weigh the pros and cons" of a decision before making a recommendation. For example, if your interviewer asks you to determine whether your client should close a plant, you can begin your answer by saying, "First I would look at the costs and benefits of this course of action," and then proceed to discuss them.

Internal vs. external market factors

This basic framework reminds you that a company's performance is affected both by its own actions and by external market factors. For example, let's say your interviewer asks you: "Our client is a major airline whose profits have fallen by half this year. Why?" You should discuss both the firm's own actions as possible causes for its drop in profits (for example, its expansion into new markets, marketing strategy, labor policies, and so on) as well as external market forces (for example, price-cutting by competitors, rising fuel prices, a tight labor market, and so on).

Fixed vs. variable costs

There are two types of costs: fixed and variable. Fixed costs are those incurred by a company month after month regardless of what it does or how much it produces (for example, rent and overhead), so they do not vary with production levels. Variable costs, on the other hand, are expenses which rise or fall depending on the company's level of production. When making decisions in the short run, only variable costs should be considered since the company can't change its fixed costs in the short run. (Note: In the long run, nearly all costs are variable, even things like rent. For example, over the long run, the firm can move to smaller offices, or even to another state or country with lower operating costs.)

A related concept is "sunk costs," or expenditures which have already been made and are not recoverable. Since sunk costs can't be recovered, they should not be factored into your decision-making. (Costs which are not yet spent or are recoverable are called "relevant costs.")

Opportunity cost

Every decision has an opportunity cost. This means simply that if you choose to do one thing, it may preclude you from doing something else. For example, if you stand in line for three hours to get a "free CD," you have in actuality "spent" on that CD whatever three hours of your time is worth. When analyzing a possible decision in a case interview, try to examine all possible opportunity costs that the subject of the case might incur by making or not making a particular decision.

Basic Overview of Financial Statements

Even if you're not an MBA, many consulting firms, especially those with strong financial consulting bents, will expect you to have some comprehension of basic financial statements. If you haven't studied accounting, don't panic – these statements are relatively easy to understand.

There are four basic financial statements that provide the information you need to evaluate a company. They include:

- The Balance Sheet
- The Income Statement
- The Statements of Retained Earnings
- The Statements of Cash Flows

In addition, a company's annual report is almost always accompanied by notes to the financial statements. These notes provide additional information about the numbers provided in the four basic financial statements.

The next four sections provide a general overview of the four basic financial statements.

The Balance Sheet

The Balance Sheet presents the financial position of a company at a given point in time. It is comprised of three parts: Assets, Liabilities and Equity. Assets are the economic resources of a company. They are the resources that the company uses to operate its business and include Cash, Inventory and Equipment. (Both financial statements and accounts in financial statements are capitalized.) A company normally obtains the resources it uses to operate its business by incurring debt, obtaining new investors, or through operating earnings. The Liabilities section of the Balance Sheet presents the debts of the company. Liabilities are the claims that creditors have on the company's resources. The Equity section of the Balance Sheet presents the net worth of a company, which equals the assets that the company owns less the debts they owe to creditors. Equity can also be defined as the claims that investors have on the company's resources.

This example uses the basic format of a Balance Sheet:

Media Entertainment, Inc Balance Sheet December 31, 2003			
Assets		**Liabilities**	
Cash	203,000	Accounts Payable	7,000
Accounts Receivable	26,000		
Building	19,000	**Equity**	
		Common Stock	10,000
		Retained Earnings	231,000
Total Assets	248,000	**Total Liabilities & Equity**	248,000

Because a company can obtain resources from both investors and creditors, one must be able to distinguish between the two and understand why one type is classified as a Liability and the other type is classified as Equity. Companies incur debt to obtain the economic resources necessary to operate their businesses and promise to pay the debt back over a specified period of time. This promise to pay is fixed and is not based upon the operating performance of the company. Companies also seek new investors to obtain economic resources. However, they don't promise to pay investors back a specified amount over a specified period of time. Instead, companies promise investors a return on their investment that is often contingent upon a certain level of operating performance. Since an equity holder's investment is not guaranteed, it is more risky in nature than a loan made by a creditor. But if a company performs well, the return to investors is often higher. The "promise-to-pay" element makes loans made by creditors a Liability and, as an accountant would say, more "senior" than equity holdings.

To summarize, the Balance Sheet represents the economic resources of a business, including the claims that creditors and equity holders have on those resources. Debts owed to creditors are more senior than the investments of equity holders and are classified as Liabilities, while equity investments are accounted for in the Equity section of the Balance Sheet.

The Income Statement

We have discussed two of the three ways in which a company normally obtains the economic resources necessary to operate its business: incurring debt and seeking new investors. A third way in which a company can obtain resources is through its own operations. The Income Statement presents the results of operations of a business over a specified period of time (e.g. one year, one quarter, one month) and is comprised of Revenues, Expenses, and Net Income.

Revenue: Revenue is a source of income that normally arises from the sale of goods or services that the company is in business to sell and is recorded when it is earned. For example, when a retailer of roller blades makes a sale, the sale would be considered revenue. However, revenue may also come from other sources. For example, selling a business segment or a piece of capital equipment generates a type of revenue for a company. This type of income would be considered a gain on sale. Gains are sources of income from peripheral or incidental transactions (all economic events that are not usual and frequent).

Expenses: Expenses are the costs incurred by a business over a specified period of time to generate the revenues earned during that same period of time. For example, in order for a manufacturing company to sell a product, it must buy the materials it needs to make the product. In addition, that same company must pay people to both make and sell the product. The company must also pay salaries to the individuals who operate the business. These are all types of expenses that a company can incur during the normal operations of the business. When a company incurs an expense outside of its normal operations, it is considered a "loss." Losses are expenses incurred as a result of one-time or incidental transactions. The destruction of office equipment in a fire, for example, would be a loss.

Incurring expenses and acquiring assets both involve the use of economic resources (i.e., cash or debt). So, when is a purchase considered an asset, and when is it considered an expense?

Assets vs. expenses: A purchase is considered an asset if it provides future economic benefit to the company, while expenses only relate to the current period. For example, monthly salaries paid to employees for services that they already provided during the month would be considered expenses. On the other hand, the purchase of a piece of manufacturing equipment would be classified as an asset, as it will probably be used to manufacture a product for more than one accounting period.

Net income: The revenue a company earns, less its expenses during a specified period of time, equals its net income. A positive net income number indicates a profit, while a negative net income number indicates that a company suffered a loss (called a "net loss").

Here is an example of an Income Statement:

Media Entertainment, Inc		
Income Statement		
(For the year ended December 31, 2003)		
Revenues		
Services Billed		100,000
Expenses		
Salaries and Wages	(33,000)	
Rent Expense	(17,000)	
Utilities Expense	(7,000)	(57,000)
Net Income		43,000

To summarize, the Income Statement measures the success of a company's operations; it provides investors and creditors with information to determine the profitability and creditworthiness of the enterprise. A company has earned net income when its total revenues exceed its total expenses. A company has a net loss when total expenses exceed total revenues.

The Statement of Retained Earnings

The Statement of Retained Earnings is a reconciliation of the Retained Earnings account from the beginning to the end of the year. When a company announces income or declares dividends, this information is reflected in the Statement of Retained Earnings. Net income increases the Retained Earnings account. Net losses and dividend payments decrease Retained Earnings.

Here is an example of a basic Statement of Retained Earnings:

Media Entertainment, Inc Statement of Retained Earnings (For the year ended December 31, 2003)	
Retained Earnings, January 1, 2003	$200,000
Plus: Net income for the year	43,000
	243,000
Less: Dividends declared	(12,000)
Retained Earnings, December 31, 2003	$ 231,000

As you can probably tell by looking at this example, the Statement of Retained Earnings doesn't provide any new information not already reflected in other financial statements. But it does provide additional information about what management is doing with the company's earnings. Management may be "plowing back" the company's net income into the business by retaining part or all of its earnings, distributing its current income to shareholders, or distributing current and accumulated income to shareholders. (Investors can use this information to align their investment strategy with the strategy of a company's management. An investor interested in growth and returns on capital may be more inclined to invest in a company that "plows back" its resources into the company for the purpose of generating additional resources. Conversely, an investor interested in receiving current income is more inclined to invest in a company that pays quarterly dividend distributions to shareholders.)

The Statement of Cash Flows

Remember that the Income Statement provides information about the economic resources involved in the operation of a company. However, the Income Statement does not provide information about the actual source and use of cash generated during its operations. That's because obtaining and using economic resources doesn't always involve cash. For example, let's say you went shopping and bought a new mountain bike on your credit card in July — but didn't pay the bill until August. Although the store did not receive cash in July, the sale would still be considered July revenue. The Statement of Cash Flows presents a detailed summary of all of the cash inflows and outflows during the period and is divided into three sections based on three types of activity:

• **Cash flows from operating activities:** includes the cash effects of transactions involved in calculating net income

• **Cash flows from investing activities:** involves items classified as assets in the Balance Sheet and includes the purchase and sale of equipment and investments

• **Cash flows from financing activities:** involves items classified as liabilities and equity in the Balance Sheet; it includes the payment of dividends as well as issuing payment of debt or equity

Here is an example that shows the basic format of the Statement of Cash Flows:

Media Entertainment, Inc
Statement of Cash Flows
For the year ended December 31, 2003

Cash flows provided from operating activities

Net Income	33,000	
Depreciation Expense	10,000	
Increase in Accounts Receivable	(26,000)	
Increase in Accounts Payable	7,000	(9,000)
Net cash provided by operating activities	24,000	

Cash flows provided from investing activities

Purchase of Building	(19,000)
Sale of Long-Term Investment	35,000
Net cash provided by investing activities	16,000

Cash flows provided from financing activities

Payment of Dividends	(12,000)
Issuance of Common Stock	10,000
Net cash provided by financing activities	(2,000)

Net increase (decrease) in cash	38,000
Cash at the beginning of the year	165,000
Cash at the end of the year	203,000

As you can tell by looking at the above example, the Statement of Cash Flows gets its information from all three of the other financial statements:

• Net income from the Income Statement is shown in the section "cash flows from operating activities."

• Dividends from the Statement of Retained Earnings is shown in the section "cash flows from financing activities."

• Investments, Accounts Payable, and other asset and liability accounts from the Balance Sheet are shown in all three sections.

Visit the Vault Consulting Career Channel at **www.vault.com/consulting** — with
insider firm profiles, message boards, the Vault Consulting Job Board and more.

VAULT CAREER LIBRARY   **33**

Advanced Concepts and Frameworks

MBAs and other candidates with business backgrounds, take note – interviewers will expect you to have a more detailed take on your case than an undergraduate would have. Here are some commonly used case concepts.

Net present value

Perhaps the most important type of decision company managers must make on a daily basis is whether to undertake a proposed investment. For example, should the company buy a certain piece of equipment? Build a particular factory? Invest in a new project? These types of decisions are called capital budgeting decisions. The consultant makes such decisions by calculating the net present value of each proposed investment and making only those investments that have positive net present values.

The net present value (or NPV) of an investment is simply the present value of the series of cash flows generated by the investment, minus the initial investment. The following example shows how to calculate NPV.

$$NPV = -C_0 + \frac{C_1}{(1 + r)} + \frac{C_2}{(1 + r)^2} + \frac{C_3}{(1 + r)^3} + ... + \frac{C_t}{(1 + r)^t}$$

Where: $C_0 =$ Initial Investment
$C_t =$ Cash flow in year t
$r =$ Discount rate

Example: *Jim Hernandez is the CFO of Western Manufacturing Corp., an automobile manufacturer. The company is considering opening a new factory in Ohio that will require an initial investment of $1 million. The company forecasts that the factory will generate after-tax cash flows of $100,000 in Year 1, $200,000 in Year 2, $400,000 in Year 3, and $400,000 in Year 4. At the end of Year 4, the company would then sell the factory for $200,000. The company uses a discount rate of 12 percent. Hernandez must determine whether the company should go ahead and build the factory. To make this decision, Hernandez must calculate the net present value of the investment. The cash flows associated with the factory are as follows:*

Year 0	Year 1	Year 2	Year 3	Year 4
-$ 1,000,000	+ $100,000	+ $200,000	+ $400,000	+ $400,000
				+$200,000 (Sell Factory)
				+ $600,000

Hernandez then calculates the NPV of the factory as follows:

$$NPV = -\$1,000,000 + \frac{100,000}{1.12} + \frac{200,000}{(1.12)^2} + \frac{400,000}{(1.12)^3} + \frac{600,000}{(1.12)^4}$$

$$= -\$1,000,000 + \$89,286 + \$159,439 + \$284,712 + \$381,311$$

$$= -\$85,252$$

Since the factory has a negative net present value, Hernandez correctly decides that the factory should not be built.

The net present value rule

Note from the example above that once the consultant has figured out the NPV of a proposed investment, she then decides whether to undertake the investment by applying the net present value rule:

Make only those investments that have a positive net present value.

As long as the consultant follows this rule, she can be confident that each investment is making a positive net contribution to the company.

The Capital Asset Pricing Model (CAPM)

In the above example, we assumed a given discount rate. However, part of a consultant's job is to determine an appropriate discount rate (r) to use when calculating net present values. The discount rate may vary depending on the investment.

Visit the Vault Consulting Career Channel at **www.vault.com/consulting** — with insider firm profiles, message boards, the Vault Consulting Job Board and more.

VAULT CAREER LIBRARY

35

Beta

The first step in arriving at an appropriate discount rate for a given investment is determining the investment's riskiness. The market risk of an investment is measured by its "beta" (ß), which measures riskiness when compared to the market as a whole. An investment with a beta of 1 has the same riskiness as the market as a whole (so, for example, when the market moves down 10 percent, the value of the investment will on average fall 10 percent as well). An investment with beta of 2 will be twice as risky as the market (so when the market falls 10 percent, the value of the investment will on average fall 20 percent).

CAPM

Once the consultant has determined the beta of a proposed investment, she can use the Capital Asset Pricing Model (CAPM) to calculate the appropriate discount rate (r):

$$r = r_f + ß(r_m - r_f)$$

$$\text{Where: } r = \text{discount rate}$$

$$r_f = \text{The risk-free rate of return}$$

$$r_m = \text{Market rate of return}$$

$$ß = \text{Beta of the investment}$$

The risk-free rate of return is the return the company could receive by making a risk-free investment (for example, by investing in U.S. Treasury bills). The market rate of return is the return the company could receive by investing in a well-diversified portfolio of stocks (for example, S&P 500).

Example: Shen, Inc., a coal producer, is considering investing in a new venture that would manufacture and market carbon filters. Shen's chief financial officer, Apelbaum, wants to calculate the NPV of the proposed venture in order to determine whether the company should make the investment. After studying the riskiness of the proposed venture, Apelbaum determines that the beta of the investment is 1.5. A U.S. Treasury note of comparable maturity currently yields 7 percent, while the return on the S&P 500 stock index is 12 percent. Therefore, the discount rate Apelbaum will use when calculating the NPV of the investment will be:

$$r = .07 + 1.5 (.12 - .07)$$
$$= .07 + .075$$
$$= .145$$
$$= 14.5\%$$

Although this is an overly simplified discussion of how consultants calculate the discount rate to use in their cash-flow analysis, it does give you an overview of how consultants incorporate the notion of an investment's market value to select the appropriate discount rate.

Porter's Five Forces

Developed by Harvard Business School professor Michael Porter in his book *Competitive Strategy*, the Porter's Five Forces framework helps determine the attractiveness of an industry. Before any company expands into new markets, divests product lines, acquires new businesses, or sells divisions, it should ask itself, "Is the industry we're entering or exiting attractive?" By using Porter's Five Forces, a company can begin to develop a thoughtful answer. Consultants frequently utilize Porter's Five Forces as a starting point to help companies evaluate industry attractiveness.

Take, for example, entry into the copy store market (like Kinko's). How attractive is the copy store market?

Potential entrants: What is the threat of new entrants into the market? Copy stores are not very expensive to open – you can conceivably open a copy store with one copier and one employee. Therefore, barriers to entry are low, so there's a high risk of potential new entrants.

Buyer power: How much bargaining power do buyers have? Copy store customers are relatively price sensitive. Between the choice of a copy store that charges 5 cents a copy and a store that charges 6 cents a copy, buyers will usually head for the cheaper store. Because copy stores are common, buyers have the leverage to bargain with copy store owners on large print jobs, threatening to take their business elsewhere. The only mitigating factors are location and hours. On the other hand, price is not the only factor. Copy stores that are willing to stay open 24 hours may be able to charge a premium, and customers may simply patronize the copy store closest to them if other locations are relatively inconvenient.

Supplier power: How much bargaining power do suppliers have? While paper prices may be on the rise, copier prices continue to fall. The skill level employees need to operate a copy shop (for basic services, like copying, collating, and so on) are relatively low as well, meaning that employees will have little bargaining power. Suppliers in this situation have low bargaining power.

Threat of substitutes: What is the risk of substitution? For basic copying jobs, more people now possess color printers at home. Additionally, fax machines have the capability to fulfill copy functions as well. Large companies will normally have their own copying facilities. However, for large-scale projects, most individuals and employees at small companies will still use the services of a copy shop. The Internet is a potential threat to copy stores as well, because some documents that formerly would be distributed in hard copy will now be posted on the Web or sent through e-mail. However, for the time being, there is still relatively strong demand for copy store services.

Competition: Competition within the industry appears to be intense. Stores often compete on price and are willing to "underbid" one another to win printing contracts. Stores continue to add new features to compete as well, such as expanding hours to 24-hour service and offering free delivery.

From this analysis, you can ascertain that copy stores are something of a commodity market. Consumers are very price-sensitive; copy stores are inexpensive to set up; and the market is relatively easy for competitors to enter. Advances in technology may reduce the size of the copy store market. Value-added services, such as late hours, convenient locations, or additional services, such as creating calendars or stickers, may help copy stores differentiate themselves. But overall, the copy store industry does not appear to be an attractive one.

PIE – The next generation of Porter's Five Forces

In their 2001 text *Strategic Management*, Garth Saloner, Andrea Shepard and Joel Podolny refined the Five Forces Model and introduced the concept of Potential Industry Earnings (PIE) to the analysis to evaluate a firm's ability to enjoy its share of the industry profits. This addition is helpful in assessing the share of profits that the group of incumbent firms retains from the total industry value.

PIE = Total value added by the industry – Total cost to produce the goods

Some industries like solar power have a high total value add to the consumer, but also an extremely high opportunity cost to produce goods. Photoelectric cells have high research and development as well as production and installation costs and therefore low PIE. The diamond industry and the designer clothing industry have significant PIE since they are able to create significant value, as shown in the prices customers are willing to pay, at a low opportunity cost.

Potential entrants

Barriers to entry such as high capital costs, proprietary technology or patents, and scale and branding of existing competitors prevent the erosion of profits by new competitors. For example, industries with low cost of entry and undifferentiated products, such as ocean fisheries that only require a boat and a small crew, mean that incumbent fisheries are not likely to capture a large share of profits unless they can create some type of barrier to new entrants such as scale or branding or some sort.

Supplier power

Suppliers are providers of the inputs to the industry being evaluated. This may include labor unions and raw materials providers, among others. Concentration of suppliers and internal competition among them determine how much leverage suppliers can have over the industry and how much of the PIE they can capture. For example, the diamond wholesaling industry depends on diamond mining and purchasing cartels to provide its inputs. A few companies control a majority of diamonds sold on the market. De Beers, one of the largest players, has pushed towards a vertical structure in which they take the diamonds to market themselves, cutting out the middle layers. The concentration of the suppliers and their power to cut off supply gives them the ability to take PIE from the diamond wholesalers and makes that industry much less attractive to a potential new competitor.

Buyer power

Buyers are the outlets for the products of the industry. The power of the buyers can take away significant PIE from incumbents. Concentration among buyers and their internal competitiveness are both determinants of buyer strength. For example, Wal-Mart and Target are very large customers of many consumer goods companies. They have a great deal of leverage over small and medium suppliers simply because of their size and scale. Not making it onto Wal-Mart's shelves can mean the difference between a successful and an unsuccessful product launch. Knowing this, Wal-Mart buyers can leverage their strength into lower wholesale prices. As a result, smaller manufacturers are not able to capture a large portion of the PIE because there are substitutes for their products.

Substitutes

The availability of acceptable substitutes can cause buyers and end customers to bypass the industry products completely and lower the size of the overall PIE. For example, at one time there were few substitutes to public pay phones; today, however, cellular phones and calling cards are considered acceptable substitutes.

Internal competition

Internal competition is usually less intense in industries in which a large portion of the market is split among one or a few large players and products are somewhat differentiated. However, these rules of thumb are not always true. For example, OPEC, the cartel of oil rich countries, has recently been able to discipline the market and raise oil prices by limiting output, but even it has been the victim of the freerider problem, with some countries secretly overselling their quota to maximize profits over the good of the whole.

Value disciplines

In 1992, the concept of value disciplines were introduced to explain how some companies are able to achieve and maintain market leadership despite being in competitive industries. By identifying what is most important for an industry and its customers, you can make specific recommendations about the direction in which a company should go.

Visit the Vault Consulting Career Channel at **www.vault.com/consulting** — with insider firm profiles, message boards, the Vault Consulting Job Board and more.

VAULT CAREER LIBRARY   **41**

Companies who surpass competitors in one of the three value disciplines can achieve success. The three value disciplines are:

1. Operational excellence

Companies who employ this value discipline focus on efficient internal operations as the means to market leadership. For example, Toyota has used its manufacturing process leadership to produce high quality cars at a relatively low cost.

2. Customer intimacy

Companies who pursue customer intimacy focus on understanding their customers' pain points and anticipating their needs. Amazon.com is one example of a company that creates a "market segment of one" for its customers by extensive recommendations and tailored marketing.

3. Product leadership

Companies that exhibit product leadership are innovators, well ahead of the technology and product curves. For example, Nokia continuously pursues leading technology and product design to meet its customer needs.

SWOT Analysis

Strength-Weakness/Opportunity-Threat Analysis is another general tool, similar to the 3Cs, for use in analyzing a company within its business environment.

The value of SWOT is in assessing how a company can use its superior capabilities to capitalize on new opportunities, while mitigating risks due to weaknesses and threats.

Strengths / Weaknesses	Used to analyze the capabilities of the company
Opportunities / Threats	Used to evaluate the company's environment

Let's take the example of Carlson Wagonlit Travel, one of the largest travel planning services in the U.S. It specializes in business travel, with some leisure components, and is often the in-house travel agency for major corporations.

Strengths

What are the company's strengths? Carlson Wagonlit has a major installed base within the corporations of the world. Its strong brand, formidable size and multinational presence are all strengths. Also, it has institutional capabilities and a network of knowledgeable employees to deliver its product.

Weaknesses

What are the company's weaknesses? Carlson Wagonlit's success fluctuates with the economy. Its business model is dependent on airline ticket commissions, which have been decreasing in recent years. Also, the company has major corporate customers who are seeking to lower their travel expenses. This can exert a great deal of price pressure on Carlson's other value-added services.

Opportunities

What opportunities does the company have? The installed base and strong brand can be leveraged into other value-added services for business and leisure travel. Additionally, it can refocus on more high-priced niche travel-planning services for which users will pay a premium.

Threats

What market threats does the company face? With the dawn of Internet travel planning, corporate employees can now find their own fares and schedules without the assistance of Carlson Wagonlit any time of day. Additionally, some companies have been experimenting with allowing employees to retain a portion of the savings for booking lower-priced, restricted travel tickets. This trend will encourage end customers to bypass corporate travel agencies and seek out the best travel plans on their own.

The SWOT framework is simple to employ and useful in trying to understand the position of a company. Based on the above SWOT analysis, Carlson Wagonlit has many important strengths that it can leverage going forward, but also faces a changing industry and revenue model. Its ability to evolve in light of these threats will be key to its long-term success.

The Seven S Framework

The Seven S Framework is a useful framework for analyzing the "internals" of a company (i.e., to determine the sources of competitive advantage for a company). The framework is a McKinsey favorite. It emphasizes that all seven "S's" are needed to form a "network" that reinforces and sustains competitive advantage. The logic is that competitors may find it possible to duplicate any one of the "S" attributes, but it will be nearly impossible to copy the complex web of interrelationships between them.

Hardware	Software
• Strategy • Structure • Systems	• Staff • Skills • Style • Shared Values

Product life cycle curve

If you're considering a product case, figure out how "mature" your product or service is.

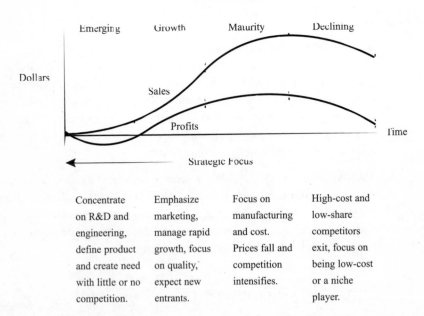

Product Life Cycle

Emerging	Growth	Maturity	Declining
Concentrate on R&D and engineering, define product and create need with little or no competition.	Emphasize marketing, manage rapid growth, focus on quality, expect new entrants.	Focus on manufacturing and cost. Prices fall and competition intensifies.	High-cost and low-share competitors exit, focus on being low-cost or a niche player.

Strategy tool/framework chart

Here's one way to think about the choice between being the lowest-cost provider or carving out a higher-end market niche – what consultants call differentiation.

Strategy	Low Cost	Differentiation
Required Capabilities	Efficient (large and dedicated) manufacturing facilities and lean overhead	Ability to identify and deliver on non-priced-based purchase criteria (strong marketing, flexible manufacturing, etc.)
Typical Markets	Commodity, low-growth, or other markets with little brand awareness or differentiation	Markets where customers purchase based on non-price factors (quality, delivery, features, etc.)
Market Timing	Mature and declining markets	Emergent (grows out of preceding market) growth and declining markets
Examples	Grain, gold, floppy disks, transportation, and temporary services	Breakfast cereal, formal attire, wine, and strategy consulting

The Four Ps

This is a useful framework for evaluating marketing cases. It can be applied to both products and services. The Four Ps consist of:

Price

The price a firm sets for its product or service can be a strategic advantage. For example, it can be predatory (set very low to undercut the competition), or it can be set slightly above market average to convey a "premium" image. Consider how pricing is being used in the context of the case presented to you.

Product

The product or service may provide a strategic advantage if it is the only product or service that satisfies a particular intersection of customer needs. Or it may simply be an extension of already existing products, and therefore not much of a benefit. Try to tease out the value of the product in the marketplace, based on the case details you have been given.

Position/Place

The physical location of a product or service can provide an advantage if it is superior to its competition, if it is easier or more convenient for people to consume, or if it makes the consumer more aware of the product or service over its competition. In the context of a business case, you may want to determine the placement of the product or service compared to its competition.

Promotion

With so much noise in today's consumer (and business to business) marketplace, it is difficult for any one product or service to stand out in a category. Promotional activity (including advertising, discounting to consumers and suppliers, celebrity appearances, etc.) can be used to create or maintain consumer awareness, open new markets, or target a specific competitor. You may want to suggest a promotional strategy in the context of the case you are presented.

The Four Cs

The Four Cs are especially useful for analyzing new product introductions and for industry analysis.

Customers

How is the market segmented?

What are the purchase criteria that customers use?

Competition

What is the market share of the clients?

What is its market position?

What is its strategy?

What is its cost position?

Do competitors have any market advantages?

Cost

What kind of economies of scale does the client have?

What is the client's experience curve?

Will increased production lower cost?

Capabilities

What resources can the client draw from?

How is the client organized?

What is the production system?

The Five Cs

This framework is mostly applied to financial cases and to companies (although it can be applied to individuals). You may employ it in other situations if you think it is appropriate.

Character

Evaluate the dedication, track record, and overall consumer perception of the company. Are there any legal actions pending against the company? If so, for what reason? Is the company progressive about its waste disposal, quality of life for its employees, and charitable contributions? What sort of impact would this have on the case you are evaluating?

Capacity

If you are dealing with a manufacturing entity, are its factories at, above, or below capacity, and for what reasons? Are there plans to add new plants, improve the technology in existing plants, or close underperforming plants? What about production overseas?

Capital

What is the company's cost of capital relative to its competitors? How healthy are its cash flows, revenues, and debt load relative to its competition?

Conditions

What is the current business climate the company (and its industry) faces? What is the short- and long-term growth potential in the industry? How is the market characterized? Is it emerging or mature? These questions can assist you in evaluating the facts of the case against the environment that the company/industry inhabits.

Competitive Advantage

This is the unique edge a company possesses over its competitors. It can be an unparalleled set of business processes, the ability to produce a product/service at a lower cost, charge a market premium, or any number of other assets that create an advantage over other market players. Whatever the case, these advantages are usually defensible and not easily copied.

In evaluating business cases using the five Cs framework, you should look for those unique qualities that a company possesses and identify any that meet the criteria mentioned above. You may suggest that the company leverage its competitive advantage more aggressively or recommend alternatives if that company has no discernible advantage.

Value chain analysis

This approach involves assessing a company's overall business processes and identifying where that company actually adds value to a product or service. The total margin of profit will be the value of the product or service to buyers, less the cost of its production, as determined by the value chain.

In most cases, a competitive advantage is only temporary for many of today's products/services. Being first to market, having a unique formula or configuration, or having exclusivity in a market were once long-term defensible strategies. But today, businesses are globally connected by lightning-fast communications and knowledge-sharing systems, and manufacturing technologies are getting better and faster at reacting to and anticipating market conditions. Thus, these advantages are fleeting, or may not exist at all.

Value chain analysis attempts to identify a competitive advantage by deconstructing the various "changes" a company's business processes perform on a set of raw materials or other inputs. Most can be easily copied by other competitors, but there is usually a unique subset that represents the "value-added" qualities only the company under scrutiny possesses. This set is that company's competitive advantage, or "value chain." Sometimes this set can be copied, but a unique set of circumstances may still allow the company in question to perform at a lower cost, charge a premium in the market, or retain higher market share than its competitors.

In the context of a business case, you can use this framework to identify a company's overall business processes set and then determine if one or more of the processes are defensible competitive advantages.

For example, a manufacturer of fruit juice might have the following value chain elements:

• Research and development (Will mango really taste good with cloudberry juice?)

• Cost of goods sold (How much does it cost to manufacture the fruit juice? Is there a frost in Florida that drives up the costs of oranges? Is the currency crisis in Indonesia making papaya very cheap? Are per-volume purchases lower than, for example, those of Tropicana?)

- Packaging and shipping (How much does that new banana-shaped container cost? Are many bottles lost in transit? What are the fixed costs of shipping?)

- Manufacturing (How much do those juice pulpers cost? How often do factories need to be reengineered?)

For more detailed information on this type of analysis, you may want to consider the authoritative text on competitive strategy: *Competitive Strategy: Techniques for Analyzing Industries and Competitors*, by Michael E. Porter.

Core competencies

"Core competencies" is the idea that each firm has a limited number of things it is very good at (that is, its core competence or competencies).

When restructuring or reengineering, one of the starting points for a company should be identifying its core competencies. A firm should define its core competencies broadly in order to be flexible enough to adapt to changes in the marketplace. (For instance, when Xerox defined itself as a "document company," rather than a maker of copy machines, it was able to take advantage of the more lucrative business of document handling and outsourcing for major corporations, as well as of the market for fax machines, scanners, and other document-handling equipment.)

Companies should seriously consider selling or spinning off business units that are not part of their "core" business. For instance, Pepsi spun off its restaurant operations after it concluded that its expertise was in manufacturing and marketing beverages, not in managing restaurants.

Benchmarking and "best practices"

A commonly used concept in consulting (especially in operations and implementation engagements) is "benchmarking." Benchmarking basically means researching what other companies in the industry are doing, usually in order to evaluate whether your client is operating efficiently, or to identify areas where the client can cut costs. For example, if a mail-order company wants to reduce its order-processing costs, it would want to compare its order processing costs with those of other mail-order companies, breaking down its costs for each part of the process (including order-taking and shipping) and comparing them with industry averages. It can then pinpoint those areas where its costs are higher than average for the industry.

A related concept is "best practices": Once you've benchmarked what other companies are doing, you want to focus on those companies that have particularly low costs or which otherwise operate particularly well. What are they doing right (i.e., what are their "best practices")? And how can our client (in the case) emulate or copy what they're doing? Remember to look outside your client's particular industry, if necessary, to find the best practices for a particular process or operation.

The 2x2 matrix

The 2x2 matrix is a good framework to use any time you have two factors that, when combined, yield different outcomes. A very rudimentary example would be what happens when you turn on your bathroom faucets, as follows:

Financing

	STOCK	DEBT
ACQUIRE	Medium Difficulty	High Difficulty
BUILD	Low Difficulty	Medium Difficulty

Acquire/Build?

A more business-appropriate example would involve acquiring a company. Let's say a company is interested in understanding the difficulty of acquiring or building a distribution center, and it is considering financing this decision with either stock or debt. The potential outcomes might look like this:

Cold Faucet

	ON	OFF
ON	Warm Water	Hot Water
OFF	Cold Water	No Water

Hot Faucet

Visit the Vault Consulting Career Channel at **www.vault.com/consulting** — with insider firm profiles, message boards, the Vault Consulting Job Board and more.

VAULT CAREER LIBRARY   51

The BCG matrix

The BCG Matrix, named after the Boston Consulting Group (BCG), is perhaps the most famous 2x2 matrix. The matrix measures a company's relative market share on the horizontal axis and its growth rate on the vertical axis.

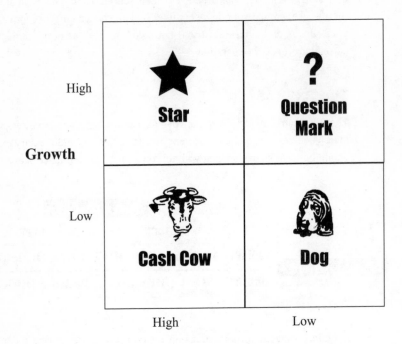

Relative Market Share (RMS)

M&A cases: Determining the drivers of value for an acquisition

Case interviews aren't just for consultants. Mergers & acquisition cases are wildly popular at investment banks. Here's how to analyze a potential acquisition.

Value Drivers (M&A) Framework

In order to understand value, we need to understand the three primary value drivers:

- Will volumes/prices increase or decrease?
- Will costs rise faster or slower than sales?
- What investments in plant and working capital are required going forward?

The value components can be further broken out into specific "value drivers":

M&A cases: Target and market assessment

The ultimate objective of a target and market assessment is to determine the value of the target.

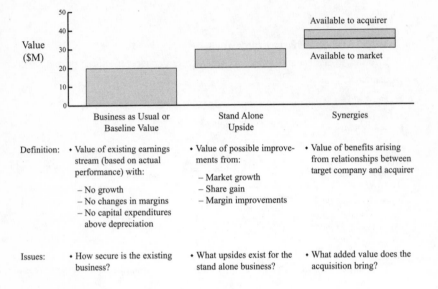

	Business as Usual or Baseline Value	Stand Alone Upside	Synergies
Definition:	• Value of existing earnings stream (based on actual performance) with: – No growth – No changes in margins – No capital expenditures above depreciation	• Value of possible improvements from: – Market growth – Share gain – Margin improvements	• Value of benefits arising from relationships between target company and acquirer
Issues:	• How secure is the existing business?	• What upsides exist for the stand alone business?	• What added value does the acquisition bring?

In assessing the factors driving value, we can determine the outlook for the target itself, as well as the market in which it competes (see next page).

	Market	**Target**
• Revenues	• What drives demand? • Is demand increasing? • What substitute products are available? • What is the outlook for prices, given supply/demand and competitive rivalry? • What is the regulatory environment?	• Why do customers buy the target's products versus those of competitors? • Will the target's market share increase or decrease? • What price premium or discount does the target command? • Is the target's market position sustainable? • What is the target's strength in supply chain?
• Costs	• Are industry costs increasing or decreasing? • Is the industry becoming increasingly competitive? • Is a technology shift likely?	• How is the target positioned versus competitor's costs? • How is the target's cost position likely to change in the future?
• Capital	• Is the business changing in a way that will require higher fixed or working capital in the future?	• How old is the target's plant? • What is its capacity? • What capital expenditures are needed for upgrades or expansion? • Is the target's working capital likely to change?

Is this an attractive business?

Is the target well-positioned in this market?

Visit the Vault Consulting Career Channel at **www.vault.com/consulting** — with insider firm profiles, message boards, the Vault Consulting Job Board and more.

V\ULT CAREER LIBRARY

55

M&A cases: Data gathering and analysis

Market Analysis Tools

• Competitive position framework

• Relative value versus competitors to customer through supply chain

• Product life cycle

• Supply and demand analysis

   – Industry capacity

   – Industry utilization

   – Demand drivers

   – Regressions

• Segmentation analysis

• Porter's Five Forces

• Experience curves

• Trends and outlook

• Key success factors

Target Analysis Tools

• Business system – comparison with competitors

• Market share (over time and by segment)

• Capacity (growth and utilization of)

• Customer's key purchase criteria and relative performance

• Financial history

• Sales and profitability by segment

• Cash flow analysis

• Margin and expense structure

• Relative cost position

• Cost benchmarking

Your data gathering strategy will vary depending on industry:

A framework caution

All the frameworks detailed above are widely used, and most business schools teach them as part of their core curriculums. Your interviewers will instantly recognize when you are applying them, since they are already familiar with the techniques. While this is fine, consider that you are trying to demonstrate your unique analytical and deductive reasoning skills that set you apart from other candidates. You must be creative and original in analyzing case questions. Use these frameworks sparingly. (Another note: No interviewer will be impressed if you proudly proclaim, "I'm going to apply Porter's Five Forces now." Apply frameworks without identifying them.)

Visit the Vault Consulting Career Channel at **www.vault.com/consulting** — with
insider firm profiles, message boards, the Vault Consulting Job Board and more.

VAULT CAREER
LIBRARY

57

How many consulting job boards have you visited lately?

(Thought so.)

Use the Internet's most targeted job search tools for consulting professionals.

Vault Consulting Job Board

The most comprehensive and convenient job board for consulting professionals. Target your search by area of consulting, function, and experience level, and find the job openings that you want. No surfing required.

VaultMatch Resume Database

Vault takes match-making to the next level: post your resume and customize your search by area of consulting, experience and more. We'll match job listings with your interests and criteria and e-mail them directly to your inbox.

BEING THERE

What It's Like Being in a Case Interview

Let's just pretend for a minute that you're Jane Candidate, and you have an interview at Boom Consulting. What might it be like? Here's what a sample 30-minute case interview might be like.

You are Jane Candidate. It's your first interview with a consulting firm. You're carefully dressed in your best navy suit (OK, so it's your roommate's best navy suit); you've charged a leather portfolio on your Visa card; and you've dutifully tucked a copy of your resume and transcript inside that glove-leather portfolio. It's time for your interview. You understand that these interviews last about half an hour.

You walk in and are greeted by Jim Interviewer, who doesn't look much older than you. In fact, you vaguely remember him from the recruitment meeting you went to in October. You shake hands firmly.

"Hi, Jane," Jim says. "It's great to meet you. Everyone on the committee was very impressed by your resume." He sounds sincere.

"I'm glad to hear it," you say, hoping you look poised and confident.

"I'm an alum of Top Ten U. myself," says Jim. "What dorm do you live in?"

"Blank House," you tell him. "How about yourself?"

After a minute of chatting about the Top Ten Pumas, Jim pulls out your resume (though you stashed a copy in your portfolio, just in case) and glances over it.

"I see you're the managing editor of the *Top Ten Tribune*," Jim says. "What was your toughest challenge as an editor?"

You talk about the *Top Ten Tribune* for a few minutes, talking about assignments you were given and the role of the newspaper at the university. At 10 after the hour, Jim looks at his watch and says, "I want to give you as much time as possible for the case. So unless you have any questions for me, let's get started."

You sit back and take a deep breath. Your case interview is about to begin!

Visit the Vault Consulting Career Channel at **www.vault.com/consulting** — with
insider firm profiles, message boards, the Vault Consulting Job Board and more.

VAULT CAREER LIBRARY

61

The Case

"Recently," says Jim, "I was at a strategy meeting with a consumer brand company. They told me that in the past two quarters, sales of their waffles rose significantly."

"Their waffles?" you interject. "I don't know a lot about breakfast food marketing, but that doesn't seem like a product that would suddenly experience a big jump in sales."

"That's right, Jane," says Jim. "That's why they asked us to look into the matter. What would you do?"

Fortunately, you've done your research on how to structure cases. You think the four Ps model might be a good way to structure this particular case. The four Ps, you recall (without looking at your note pad), are price, position, promotion and product.

You tell Jim how you're going to proceed with your analysis.

"Let's break down the situation like this. First, I'm going to try to find out about the market position of the waffles. Then, I'm going to try to figure out how the waffles are being promoted. After that, I'll ask whether there are any price-based reasons for the surge in waffle sales. Finally, I'll ask you about the waffles themselves."

"That seems like a reasonable way to proceed," comments Jim.

"Okay, then," you say. "What is the overall market for waffles? Has it grown recently?"

"No," says Jim. "Demand for waffles seems to be holding steady."

"That means we're taking our waffle sales from other waffle manufacturers."

"It seems so," confirms Jim.

"Is there a seasonal reason for this increase in waffle consumption? Perhaps people eat more waffles when it's cold?"

"No, our waffles sales are normally steady year-round."

"Have sales of other breakfast foods or our own breakfast products increased as well?"

"No, they haven't," says Jim. "There seems to be no uptick in the breakfast food market."

"Has our client entered any new markets recently? Perhaps they've entered the Asian market? I'm assuming that these waffles are only sold in North American markets."

"Your assumption is correct, and that is a good question," says Jim. "In fact, the company does plan to expand into the European and Asian markets. That's why they want to know the reason behind the sales upsurge – so they can replicate it. But for the time being, no, they haven't expanded the sales area."

You're getting a little frustrated, but so far, Jim hasn't indicated that your reasoning is unsound.

"Okay, let's talk about promotion and price," you say. "Has our client lowered prices recently?"

"No," says Jim.

"Have other waffle manufacturers raised their prices?"

"Nope," says Jim.

"Is our product a premium product – have we raised prices?"

"No," says Jim. "There is little price differential between our waffles and competing waffle products. And prices have not varied in the past two quarters. In fact, our waffles are slightly more expensive than some waffles and a bit less than others."

You get the feeling that Jim is telling you to back off the price issue.

"Then maybe there's some kind of promotion going on. Has the company started advertising its waffles? Is it promoting a related product, like syrup?"

Jim answers no to both.

"Maybe the price of all syrup has gone down?" you guess.

"That would affect the consumption of all waffles," says Jim.

You guess blindly: "Is there a celebrity who's recently become famous for eating our waffles?"

Jim laughs. "That's not it."

"Then tell me about our client's promotion process," you say.

Visit the Vault Consulting Career Channel at **www.vault.com/consulting** — with
insider firm profiles, message boards, the Vault Consulting Job Board and more.

VAULT CAREER LIBRARY

63

"Our client spends about $10 million yearly on waffle promotion. Every month, we run advertisements in three selected magazines. We also have coupon promotions and a commercial that runs on TV."

Now, you think, you're on to something! "Have we started to put our commercials on more popular programs? Has the quality of our advertising improved?"

To your frustration, Jim shakes his head. "We haven't significantly changed our promotion campaign. The ratings of the shows we advertise on are about the same. We have noticed more use of our coupons, however."

"Has the demographic of our advertising changed?" you ask. "Is the client now pitching to people who are more likely to eat waffles?"

"As far as we can tell, the makeup and audience of our advertising targets hasn't changed," says Jim.

You're determined to uncover the reason behind this waffle case – and you don't have that much time left. "Then perhaps something has changed about our product," you say. "Has the shape changed?"

"Well," says Jim, "it has changed a bit."

"How so?"

"It's flattened out somewhat."

"Why? Has the production process changed?"

"Yes, it has," says Jim. "We're using a new template for the waffles as part of a general factory modernization."

"Are the ingredients the same?"

"Those have changed too. We're using a new supplier."

"Then," you say, "I would venture to guess that consumers in North America prefer a flatter, larger waffle. There must be something about the new production process that has created a better waffle."

"Yes," says Jim. "Our focus groups show that the texture and crispiness of the waffle has improved. Consumers are responding to our inadvertently improved waffle."

"Then I recommend that we investigate whether European and Asian markets would respond in a similar manner to our new waffle product. We should also promote our waffle advantage in the market. Perhaps we could enter new markets for waffles, like using them for dinner, as crepes."

"Your suggestions are interesting, and we'll look at them later," says Jim. "Good job! Do you have any questions for me about Boom Consulting?"

REAL LIFE
INTERVIEWS

There's no substitute for experience. Read on for some from-the-trenches accounts of real-life consulting interviews. Please keep in mind that these are the unique experiences of individuals and should not be construed as the typical case experience in any consulting firm. Consulting interviews may vary by office and interviewer.

Boston Consulting Group, MBA

I had five case interviews at BCG and two regular interviews. What was unusual was that two different people asked me to look at data and charts and talk about what was said, as opposed to talking about a case per se. That's a typically unusual BCG thing to do. They'd show you, for example, a data table and a graph.

One of my cases was about a content syndication company, and one was about a paper company that was becoming less profitable. (Apparently a lot of cases are about paper companies, because they're big business but no one knows anything about them offhand.) You should think about revenue and fixed versus variable costs.

Sometimes cases are not set in the present day. I had one case set in 1985, specifically so I couldn't offer Internet solutions.

Another case was about a pharmaceutical company trying to go online. The case asked what the best way would be to determine which services you put online and which you wouldn't. You have to think about who the customers were and the supply chain — basically, the four Ps.

I found BCG consultants to be friendly — my interviews were more like discussions. In one instance, I had trouble with a data chart. I asked for help and got good hints. I suggest that you stop in the beginning of the BCG case and take notes or you will get lost. The case is usually 20 to 25 minutes.

Visit the Vault Consulting Career Channel at **www.vault.com/consulting** — with
insider firm profiles, message boards, the Vault Consulting Job Board and more.

VAULT CAREER LIBRARY

69

McKinsey & Company, MBA

I had six case interviews with McKinsey.

I found, and it was the experience of my fellow MBA students interviewing as well, that the cases at McKinsey are very quantitative. A lot of cases at McKinsey were about estimating market size, and there is sometimes difficult math. I struggled a little bit with some of the calculations, and they would throw something in to speed things up, like "Oh, why don't we just say 20 million." On the other hand, I had one interview where I had two market sizings, and you were only supposed to have one. I solved it too fast, so I got another one.

I had to estimate the size of the restaurant market in New York City and estimate the number of cars produced on an assembly line every day. That was complicated. I had to calculate how quickly the conveyor belt was moving, the schedule of the factory, etc. Sometimes they would add new information, like "Let's say the factory is closed on Sunday."

I also had a few others. Here was one case: You have five million dollars. You can buy a building in New York City or you can invest it at 7 percent return. It's a discounted cash flow problem. You had to determine what kind of building it was, what kind of location, what the income was from rental, estimate the volatility of the real estate market.

I also had the question "What will your phone bill look like in five years?"

Keep in mind that you're being watched every minute you're in the office. I know some people who discussed their cases while they were in the bathroom. They didn't get an offer.

Monitor Group, undergraduate

Monitor has a weird case process. They have a written case they give you with a lot of data and numbers. There are four specific questions you have to answer, some of them quantitative. They do allow you to have a calculator. Afterwards, you talk through your answers. Mine was a manufacturer, its market size, its main competitors, and how it should increase their revenues.

The final round is a group interview. You get data and are asked to pull qualitative data out. You have half an hour to look at the problem and develop a quick presentation to the whole group. Then you talk about the presentation together, like you were an engagement team. Everyone was pretty cautious. They didn't know whether or not to be aggressive. In general, everyone was friendly or supportive. Afterwards, they show you a staged presentation of a client-consultant situation and ask you for your feedback and what you would have done in the same situation.

A.T. Kearney, undergraduate

My experience was atypical. [A.T. Kearney] doesn't have a lot of people at the undergraduate level, and they are very top-heavy. They described it to me as an inverted pyramid. At the first interview, I didn't have a case. I was asked about where I saw A.T. Kearney fitting into the consulting scheme of things. They are very interested in differentiating themselves. I had one interview where I was given a lot of information that essentially said that Internet companies were all overvalued and that to justify their valuations a virtually impossible number of people would need to get online. Then she asked me what I thought. I think she just wanted to see how much I knew about the Internet economy.

I had one case with a manufacturer of computer products. I had to figure out how to save them ten million dollars. After asking a lot of questions, the key takeaway was that they had a lot of computers on the shelf. They needed to speed up the manufacturing and shipping process. That's because computers lose value very quickly.

I had another interview that was also about computer manufacturers. It was about a company trying to get into selling services. I had to identify key points for the business plan.

L.E.K. Consulting, MBA

I had two cases in the first round. One was fit and the second one was a case interview. The interviewer just looked at me and said, "I've been thinking a lot about the Web boxes on televisions. What are some of your thoughts about their viability?" They really wanted to see if you knew anything about the tech market.

In my second case, I was given a lot of different scenarios about a generic sort of company, and we had to draw a lot of graphs. They would say things like, "We have a cost structure where it's variable up until a certain point, but after that it's fixed, and we have these costs. Okay, what if you took out variable costs?" It was all about the line graph.

In the second round, I met with managers [senior consultants]. I had a neat case about the Internet. It was thinking about the advantages and disadvantages of moving operations online if you're a bricks-and-mortar retailer. They wanted to make sure that I understood current events about technology and that the Internet company isn't always linked with the parent company. We talked about Nordstrom.com for a while.

In the second half of the interview, I was asked to explain anything I was passionate about.

I was also asked a lot of questions about Excel and the most advanced thing I had done on Excel, which I found odd.

BUSINESS CASES

The following is a sampling of business case questions. Some are provided with suggested answers or lines of reasoning. Remember that there is no right answer to these questions, so what follows each question is a suggested outline or framework for working through your solution. You may use any line of reasoning you are comfortable with, but remember to be concise and confident, and to make NO assumptions. If you don't have enough facts to move forward, ask! Only if your interviewer refuses to give you information should you make sensible assumptions – while informing the interviewer that you're making them. Sketching out a few graphs may help clarify your analysis (and impress your interviewer, as graphs are the coin of the consulting trade). Increasingly, interviewers may ask you to interpret data or graphs as part of your case.

Case Formats

Readers may observe that the format of these cases differs slightly. Here's a description of how these cases differ and how to use them for your case research.

Some of these cases simulate the conversation between the interviewer and the candidate. These cases are meant to give you an idea of what a good response to the interviewer in a case situation.

Other cases, instead of a sample interviewer/candidate conversation, include a detailed analysis of the case question. This allows you to see a broader cross-section of case analysis.

You will also find some additional practice cases. Some of these include a point of jumping-off analysis, while others are blank.

Finally, in this edition for the first time we include interactive cases. These cases are designed for you to practice with another person. If you use all the interactive cases and want to try some more, the additional practice cases make great additional interactive cases.

Visit the Vault Consulting Career Channel at **www.vault.com/consulting** — with
insider firm profiles, message boards, the Vault Consulting Job Board and more.

VAULT CAREER LIBRARY

75

Practice Questions

1. Leaving on a Jet Plane

A major airline is considering the purchase of 24 new planes. They are unclear how this purchase will affect their business performance in the short term as well as the long term. You are the Senior Consultant, meeting with the Operating Committee for the first time. I am the Chief Operating Officer of the company. What would you need to know from me in order to assess the situation?

Here is a good example of a directed question combined with a role-playing exercise. Not only will the interviewer be assessing your analysis and deductive abilities, but she will also be evaluating your poise and professionalism in front of a senior executive. In many cases, consultants find themselves in front of key client personnel who are older and more experienced in the industry, so your ability to cope with this type of situation is essential. How will you actually go about assessing the situation and finding information once you arrive at the client? (This case was given to an MBA-level candidate.)

You: What is the planned delivery cycle of the new aircraft? Will it be staggered, serial, or all at once?

Interviewer: Aircraft will be delivered as they are manufactured over the next five years, at approximately four per year.

You: How many planes are in the current fleet? Are there any plans to sell off older aircraft as the newer aircraft are delivered?

Interviewer: There are 120 planes in the current fleet. There are no plans to get rid of our older aircraft as the new ones arrive.

You: What is the current average cost per flight-hour of the fleet?

Interviewer: It varies by aircraft type. The range is anywhere from $1,000 to $5,000.

You:	Do you have any frameworks in mind for assessing this situation?
Interviewer:	No. What would you suggest? (This is a tough response because it asks you to put a stake in the ground.)
You:	Well, in many cases I have used a company's cost of capital, relative to the average cost of capital in the industry, industry-specific metrics like the cost per flight-hour, as I already mentioned, and depreciation method choice. I would also want to assess the new efficiencies brought about by your purchase, as in fuel cost savings, increased passenger load, and so on. Do these sound reasonable to you?
Interviewer:	Yes, as a beginning. How will you go about finding the information you need?
You:	I would first need to know appropriate contact people in purchasing, finance, and accounting who could provide the quantitative facts I need to perform the assessment. With your introduction, I would like to meet with each of these people, from two hours to a half-day, in order to gather the information. I would need to circle back through each of them after the initial interviews simply to validate the information I have compiled, once I have assembled a draft.
Interviewer:	That sounds like a workable plan.

2. Help! Our Profit Margins are Shrinking!

You are the consultant to a company that produces large household appliances. Over the past three years, profit margins have fallen 20 percent and market share has tumbled to 15 percent of the market from 25 percent. What is the source of the company's problems?

This is an example of the type of question an undergraduate student (or an MBA student in an early interview round) might receive. The interviewer has done you the favor of defining the problem – your client is in something of a slump! This dialogue illustrates how you, the perspicacious candidate, might drill down into the core of the woes besetting the firm.

You:	How would you characterize the current marketplace for these products? Emerging? Mature?
Interviewer:	The product line is considered mature.
You:	How would you characterize your manufacturing process relative to your competition? (You're looking to see if the company has a strategic advantage.)
Interviewer:	Can you be more specific?
You:	Do you benefit from an advantage in technology, economies of scale, exchange rates, or other manufacturing element over your competition?
Interviewer:	We have not updated our manufacturing process since 1988. We manufacture our products exclusively in the United States. As one of the oldest manufacturers of these products, we have a reliable customer base and a good reputation. As for price, we are one of the lower-priced in the market, though not the lowest.
You:	Do any of your competitors manufacture overseas?
Interviewer:	Our number one competitor produces all of its appliances in Indonesia. (Here's your clue – manufacturing outside the country significantly lowers costs.)
You:	It probably suffices to say that some of your decline in profit can be attributed to the increased costs you are facing relative to older manufacturing techniques and higher costs associated with manufacturing domestically. This is especially troublesome in a mature market where consumers are mostly aware of the product category and the product may be considered a commodity. (A commodity marketplace is one in which customers make their purchasing decisions largely on price. For example, toilet paper is largely a commodity market, where consumers buy whatever's on sale.)
	Let's talk about market share now. Can you tell me about any recent market research you have regarding the strength of your brand, price, your products' position, and any promotional activity you have had?

Interviewer:	Our market research department has told us that consumers are confused about the product category, that they do not understand the differences between our brand and our competitors' brands. We sell to all major appliance retailers in the U.S. We promote aggressively twice a year and have smaller promotions once a quarter. (This is consistent with the description of a commodity product. The ways of breaking out of commodity markets include promotions and making value-added differences in the brand – like, in the case of toilet paper, introducing new designer colors and specially quilted cotton-blend paper.)
You:	What form does your promotional activity take?
Interviewer:	We offer a price discount to consumers twice a year. We regularly advertise in major magazines targeted to our consumer, and we have an active outdoor campaign underway.
You:	It would appear you are competing in an undifferentiated marketplace, and there may be an opportunity to capture additional share through an aggressive brand differentiation effort. I believe it would also be worth investigating the efficacy of your current promotional programs, relative to your competition. The consumer may be responsive to other types of promotions that haven't been utilized by the company as of yet.

3. Banking on Savings

A bank is trying to increase its operating efficiency. Your consulting team has been asked to look at the non-interest, non-personnel expense base in order to cut costs. How would you determine the potential size of the opportunity for operating efficiency? What issues might arise in such a study?

This is an exercise in full-value procurement (FVP). FVP is a rationalization across business units of common purchases and services. The measure of an FVP is the amount of "spend" reduced, defined as the cost savings realized by reducing the number of sources from which common products/services are purchased. (This question, and questions like it that require advanced frameworks, are much more likely to be received by business school candidates and case interviewees with significant business experience than by undergraduates with no business experience.)

In this case interview, your interviewer will impersonate the client. Case interviews often take this kind of role-playing form (which can be fun!).

You:	What is your revenue level on an annual basis like?
Interviewer:	In 1998 our revenues were $1.2 billion. (These seem to be the revenues of a prosperous regional bank, not a bulge bracket.)
You:	What are the common items and services that all business units use? Do you have common office suppliers or housekeeping services?
Interviewer:	Well, obviously we have most common office products shared across all our functions. We also have cleaning services for our corporate headquarters, our printing center, and our retail locations.
You:	How many vendors provide similar products and services to the bank?
Interviewer:	We buy office products from OfficeMax's corporate services in Indiana, Avery Dennison corporate services in California, and someone else, the name of which escapes me right now, for the retail banks. Also, I believe we contract regionally for housekeeping services.
You:	Is consolidating branch offices or reducing ATM counts a possibility?
Interviewer:	Not at this time. In fact, we're planning to expand in three different states.
You:	Are your cost concerns the result of an impending merger? (Perhaps the interviewer has deliberately left out an important piece of information – the bank has undergone, or is planning, a merger or acquisition of another bank that might drive up costs.)

Interviewer:	No, our growth is organic, not through acquisition. (Looks like this is a dead end. Time to move on to other considerations.)
You:	Have you considered outsourcing non-critical business tasks?
Interviewer:	What kind do you suggest? (Your interviewer is probing to see if you can name the kind of services a bank might successfully outsource.)
You:	Well, what about information systems, call centers and customer service, bill collection, document handling, those kind of things?
Interviewer:	Oh, no. That's not possible. (Remember that this is a role play. This seems a bit uncommunicative for a reasonable suggestion; you should probe a bit further. Businesses aren't always entirely reasonable in their actions!)
You:	Can you explain your objections?
Interviewer:	Don't you think outsourcing those processes is extreme? We're a bank, and we have a lot of confidential information on both paper and electronic media. Our integrity would be put at risk if we let others manage our internal functions.
You:	Well, sir, I understand your objections. However, many major corporations use organizations that centralize activities like copy centers and conference planning, all of which also have trade secrets and confidential information.
Interviewer:	That sounds interesting, and I'd like more information. (Your interviewer graciously acknowledges the wisdom of your suggestions.) But can you give me a concrete suggestion my supervisor will like?
You:	(Time to return to a less controversial aspect.) What would you estimate your spending to be for things like office products?

Interviewer:	I estimate about $100 million on office products, corporation wide, in 1998, though you'd have to talk to our operations people, of course.
You:	I think, based on your information, that there are ample opportunities for cost savings that I can identify right now. Reducing your vendors down to one or two will allow you to use economies of scale to extract cost savings. Outsourcing promises even greater savings.

4. Paper or Air

A restaurant owner is currently setting up a new restaurant and making some basic decisions on how to fit it out. Today he is making a decision on the facilities to place in the restrooms for customers to dry their hands. Initial research suggests that he has three options – paper towels, roller towels and hot air dryers. What should he consider in his decision-making process?

In the initial analysis, you might ask a number of questions, which will influence your decision.

- What type of restaurant is it going to be – luxurious, budget, middle-market?

- How many customers does he expect? How many tables? Is it open during the day? In the evening?

- Has he done any customer research to see what customers would prefer?

Fairly soon in the process, you should start asking questions about the economics of the three options – in which case the interviewer will give you some more information:

In the initial research, the restaurant owner has found out the following information from the suppliers of the drying facilities:

- Dryers have an initial cost of $500 each (but you'll need two – one for each restroom) and monthly service charge of $100 per month. The supplier estimates that the lifetime of a dryer is four years.

- Paper towels cost 5 cents each, and the number of paper towels that you will need varies directly with the number of customers. So if you expect 50 customers a night, they will use 50 towels.

- If you use toweling rolls, they will cost $5 per roll (and again you'll need two – one for each restroom). The rolls will be changed daily if the restaurant has more than 2,000 customers per month or every other day if there are less than 2,000 customers per month.

At this point, it's obvious that from an economic standpoint, the option you select will vary with the number of customers. Therefore, it makes sense to look at a break-even calculation.

First of all, take the dryers. They cost $100 per month, plus an upfront charge of $1,000 that you should depreciate over their lifetime (i.e. an additional $1,000/(4 x 12) per month = $21 per month). Therefore their total cost is approximately $120 per month – and this does not vary with the number of customers coming into the restaurant.

Secondly, look at the paper towels option. These vary directly with the number of customers in the restaurant, at a cost of $0.05 per customer. Therefore, with a low number of customers per month, paper towels will be cheaper than dryers will. How many customers would have to come to the restaurant each month to make the dryers more cost effective? The cost of towels would have to exceed $120 per month, equating to $120/$0.05 = 2,400 customers per month.

Is this break-even affected by the rolls option? At less than 2,000 customers per month, the rolls would cost $10 every other day or $10 x 15 days = $150 per month. This in itself is more costly than both the dryer and the towels option, and with more than 2,000 customers, it will only look more unfavorable.

Therefore the real economic decision is between towels and dryers. At less than 2,400 customers per month (or 2,400/30 = 80 customers per night) you would prefer the towels. Once the number of customers increases above this, you'd switch to the dryers' option.

Following the economic analysis, you might mention a few more non-economic points that might sway the balance:

- Are there additional staff costs of cleaning up paper towel waste?

- How many suppliers of each option are there? If there is a single supplier, might he have the capacity to raise prices in the future?

Hints on quantitative cases:

- Make the numbers easy – round up or down when possible to make further calculations easier.

- When you're jotting down numbers, make sure you keep a track of what is what, so when you pull together your recommendations at the end of the analysis, you can make comparisons between the options.

- In break-even cases, it is sometimes effective to draw a graph to illustrate the break-even decision (in this case, number of customers per month along the x-axis vs. cost of drying option along the y-axis).

5. Making a Case out of Lemons

Your niece approaches you and says, "Since you're a management consultant, maybe you can help me. I want to buy my mother a present for her birthday, and I was thinking of opening a lemonade stand to earn the money. Tell me what you think of my plan."

Isn't she cute? Yet this is a serious case (from Bain, no less). The interviewer is trying to see if you can set up a value chain for your niece. Get out your notepad.

You:	What kind of present do you want to get for your mother?
Interviewer:	I want to get her a pair of gold earrings.
You:	That's a very nice idea. I'm going to assume that you want to buy a pair of earrings that cost $50.
Interviewer:	Actually, the earrings I want cost $100. (The interviewer is trying to raise the bar a bit.)
You:	Okay. When is your mom's birthday? What's your timeframe?
Interviewer:	My mother's birthday is in three months.
You:	What kind of time commitment can you make to the lemonade stand? How many days a week do you plan to run the stand?

Interviewer: I have to go to school during the week, so I think just on weekends.

You: Here are some of the considerations you need to make if you want to earn $100 in three months from your lemonade stand.

What are your expenses? Let's say that you need to buy the pitcher, which is $2. Every 100 plastic cups will cost you $1 in direct costs. Those are your base expenses.

You then have to make several cost decisions. What size cups will you use? Eight-ounce cups will mean that you can serve more cups of lemonade per pitcher. (If it's a gallon jug, with 64 ounces, then you can serve eight cups per pitcher. Sixteen-ounce cups, which may be perceived as a better value, means that you can serve only four per pitcher.)

You must also decide what kind of lemonade to serve. Lemonade made from powdered concentrate is probably the cheapest – perhaps $1 a gallon. Lemonade made from fresh squeezed lemons has a definite quality advantage, but it's more expensive. At $0.25 a lemon and eight lemons to a gallon, it would cost $2 for each gallon. And you might be able to get prepackaged lemonade sold at the store for $1.50 a gallon.

Interviewer: So how long will it take me to get enough money for the earrings?

You: Assume $10 in sunk costs – $2 for the pitcher and $8 for 800 cups. You then need to decide what to charge. If you charge 50 cents a cup of lemonade – which I believe is the upward end of lemonade stand prices – and it costs you $1 to make the cheapest gallon of lemonade, then you'd earn $3 on each gallon of lemonade sold. In four weekends in three months, you would need to sell 37 gallons of lemonade. Then you'd earn $111 dollars – enough to pay off the pitcher and cups. That's three gallons a weekend, or 24 cups of lemonade each weekend.

Interviewer: Does this sound reasonable to you?

You:	So far, yes. But this is just the cost structure. You must consider other factors as well. Who are your competitors? Are there other kids trying to sell lemonade at the same time? Are you located near delis and restaurants and street vendors who might sell competing beverages?

What is the demand for your product? Is it summertime, when people drink a lot of lemonade and are spending time outdoors, generating foot traffic? If not, you may have difficulty moving your lemonade. In cold weather, you might want to consider selling hot cider instead.

Where are you located? How many potential customers will pass your lemonade stand? Can you set up your lemonade stand at a sporting event, supermarket parking lot, or flea market, where many more people will pass your stand? If you just set up on the sidewalk, you may not attract the foot traffic to make those numbers. Indoor or sheltered locations are also preferable if the weather turns bad.

You have a competitive advantage – you're young and cute. You may get business from people who approve of your young entrepreneurial actions. At the same time, lemonade stands have a reputation for relatively poor lemonade, which may hurt your overall sales if you have competition.

Do you have any subsidies? That is, would your dad be willing to cover your start-up costs – the pitcher, the cups, and perhaps the cost of the lemonade? This would perhaps permit you to offer better-quality lemonade, which might be important to your customers.

Consider your advertising. You'll need a big sign to call attention to your stand. You can rely on your parents for free – I assume – word of mouth.

You should also consider offering another product besides lemonade. Perhaps selling cookies or brownies, in addition to the lemonade, might increase your profits.

You should consider other revenue-generating activities as well. If you are 14, a paper route is a possibility. You may also be old enough to babysit.

It's also possible that you might be able to choose another pair of earrings or find the ones you want on sale. This would lower your income requirements.

6. Phoning in a Case

You are advising a credit card company that wants to market a prepaid phone card to its customers. Is this a good idea?

Whoa! Better find out more about this prepaid phone card first before you even begin to think about recommending it.

You: What is the role of our company? Do we simply market the card or must we create them ourselves? Are we expected to provide the telephone services?

Interviewer: This card will be co-marketed with an outside phone company. We do not need to perform telecommunications functions.

You: What are our expenses connected with the card?

Interviewer: We must pay 15 cents for every minute we sell. We also have to pay $1.00 as a start-up cost for the card and card systems.

You: What are our marketing expenses?

Interviewer: We normally use slips of paper that are attached to the backs of our credit card payment envelopes. We sometimes also send customers a direct mailing – in a separate envelope. Or we can have telemarketers call selected customers.

You: What's the cost of each of these marketing techniques, and what is their response rate?

Interviewer: Telemarketers have a 2 percent response rate and cost $1.00 per call. Direct mailings cost us 40 cents per mailing and have a 0.50 percent rate of response. Our payment attachments have a 0.25 percent rate of response, but only cost us 5 cents each.

You: I'm going to assume we will sell one-hour phone cards. That will cost us $9.00 for the minutes and a dollar per card – so each card costs us $10.

Interviewer: Okay, that sounds reasonable.

You: And what is our expected revenue on a one-hour phone card? What is the current market rate for a 60-minute phone card?

Interviewer: Assume it's 50 cents a minute.

You: So if we sell the cards for $30, we have a $20 profit, minus our expenditures on marketing.

Interviewer: What's our cost structure look like?

You: Okay, let's figure this out. To sell 1,000 cards through telemarketing, we would need to contact 50,000 people. That would cost us $50,000. To use direct mail, we would have to contact 200,000 thousand people, which, at 40 cents per mailing, costs us $80,000. Since the envelope inserts aren't very reliable, we will need to contact 800,000 people using that method. But at 5 cents each, it costs only $20,000 to sell 1,000 cards.

We make $20 profit on each card. But even using the cheapest promotional vehicle, at $20 profit, we would only break even, because our profits on 1,000 cards would be $20,000. We shouldn't market this card, unless we can further cut our marketing costs or increase the price of the card. If we could slice the cost of the envelope attachments a penny or so, or sell the card for $35, or convince our co-marketer to reduce our costs, it might be worth selling.

Interviewer: What are some other issues you might want to consider? (Notice how the interviewer is nudging you to add to your analysis.)

You: We should also consider the competitive landscape for this business. Is the per-minute rate for calling card minutes expected to fall? If so, and our costs are held constant, we may lose money. Of course, we can learn more from marketing these cards. It could be that the people likely to buy these cards might be frequent travelers and could be targeted for other promotions.

Thinking Strategically

7. Beam Me Up!

The Star Trek transporter has just been invented. Spell out some of the effects on the transportation industry.

Here's another (actual) case which calls for strategy analysis. First of all, remember not to make any assumptions. Don't apologize for not watching the show – ask your interviewer (who, if she or he has given you this question, is probably a fan) how exactly the transporter works. Effectively, the transporter is a near-instantaneous teleportation device. However, you should make sure you don't assume exactly what the transporter, as invented, can or can't do. (In this case, non-Trekkies may have an advantage!)

Let's see how this Q&A might proceed:

You: Could you tell me exactly how the transporter works? How much can it transport at one time?

Interviewer: Let's say the transporter can transport about the mass of Captain Kirk.

You: That would be about 200 pounds. Can it transport only living things, or inanimate objects as well?

Interviewer: Any type of object.

You: Can it transport anywhere at any time?

Interviewer: Yes.

You: Does there need to be another transporter at the end to receive the transport?

Interviewer: No, it's pretty much a one-way process.

You: How common are these devices? Are they going to be readily available to the average consumer? How much do they cost?

Interviewer: For the time being, the transporters are expensive. They would cost about $100,000 each.

You: That clearly takes them out of the range of most home users. How much does it cost to use them?

Interviewer: Assume that the marginal cost of a transport is near zero. The only cost is for the transport-operator time, which is relatively small.

You: Are they safe? You said they were just invented.

Interviewer: Except for the occasional freak accident, yes, they are safe. They are as safe as plane travel.

You: That makes them very safe indeed. Okay, what I'm going to do is analyze how transporters will affect the following transportation industries: cars, passenger airlines, cargo shipping and package transport.

Interviewer: Fine. Go ahead.

You: These transporters don't seem like they'll take the place of cars. They are too expensive for home use. Larger companies could afford them, however. I could see some companies buying transporters in order to transport their employees and clients back from the office. They would need a transporter chief, of course. So there might be some impact on commuter traffic – perhaps 10 to 20 percent. If mass transit systems adopt transporters as well, the impact on traffic may be greater.

On the other hand, the transporter is a terrific substitute for plane travel. It's instantaneous and from what you say, as safe as plane travel. The transporter will definitely be a serious competitor to airlines. Conceivably, passengers could be beamed directly to their destination, instead of going to the airport. The only drawback that I can see to the transporter is that any luggage would need to be beamed separately. And anyone weighing over 200 pounds may not be able to be beamed at all. This means that airplanes wouldn't disappear, but they would be used mostly for cargo transport and other heavier loads. They would probably serve fewer markets, as there would be much-reduced passenger travel to supplement their flights.

As far as cargo, I think ships and planes would still be used for most cargo transport. Two hundred pounds is too small an amount for mass transport, and I'm assuming that you can't separate the contents of a transporter, that you can only beam stuff to one area at once.

Interviewer: That's how I understand it, yes.

You: Then getting packages sent same day, to anywhere in the world, would be a premium service. You could only ship one package at a time. You might be able to charge double or triple the price of an overnight package. Shipping companies like Federal Express might profit from its introduction.

Using the Four Ps

8. Taking Wing

It's 1982. You're a consultant sitting on the plane next to your client, who is the CEO of American Airlines. The client tells you that American can't seem to keep many repeat customers and wants to institute something called a "frequent flyer" program to reward loyal passengers with "points" they can redeem for free flights. He turns to you and asks you to analyze the merits and faults of the program. How do you respond?

This is a good candidate for the Four Ps framework. (Note that the interviewer has deliberately set this case at a time when you cannot use online membership as a substitute or addition.) A good analysis would kick off with some scoping questions to understand the evolution of the idea:

- Are you aware of any programs currently in existence that caused you to consider this idea for American Airlines? If so, what do you feel are major advantages/disadvantages?

- Have you done any market research within your customer base to determine how well this program would be received if instituted?

- Can you sketch the purchasing habits of your top flyers for me? How much do they currently spend on air travel per year, what percentage is business vs. leisure, are there a particular set of routes this group frequents, do they stick with one airline or purchase tickets on many airlines, etc.?

- Would the current customer service business unit be charged with implementing this program or would you consider investment in a separate initiative?

Price

- Would there be a membership fee for this program? Would this program be available to all American customers or only those who fly at or over a certain threshold?

- Based on your customers' current flight habits, would you set milestones for award redemption?

Product

- Would the program be based on miles, segments, price of tickets, or another factor?

- What need would this program satisfy that does not currently exist in the marketplace?

- Would there be any redemption restrictions based on route or day?

- What other rewards would be available to members besides flights? Special member lounges in airports? Car rentals? Hotel rooms?

- What would be accumulated – points, miles, levels?

- Would these accumulated criteria ever expire?

- Would you award extremely high-volume flyers with additional perks? What would they be? Would flyers have to re-earn this status or, once attained, would it be good for life?

Position/Place

- Are you aware of any similar programs in today's marketplace? If so, what would differentiate your program from others that already exist?

- Based on your knowledge of your customers' behavior, would you think that a frequent flyer program would induce high switching costs, such that it would make it difficult for high-volume customers to switch airlines due to the loss of miles/status with American?

Promotion

- How would you introduce this program to your customers? Through airports, the media, travel agents? Would it be available only to frequent flyers or all the flying public?

- How would customers sign up for this program? Would it be automatic, a form, a phone call to customer service?

- Would there ever be any promotional drives such as doubling awards or offering bundle pricing (such as two-for-one)?

Be careful of using historic precedent in historic cases. While frequent flyer miles are a fact of business history, your analysis might show that the long-term benefits are not worth the creation of the program.

Sailing the Five Cs

9. You have the opportunity to purchase a landscaping business. How would you decide whether or not to buy it, and how much to pay for it?

This question is a good candidate for the Five Cs. Determine:

Character
- How would you evaluate the sincerity, honesty, and integrity of the owner of the business? Do others that they deal with (employees, suppliers, customers) value them as partners, or are there character issues?

- Is there any legal action pending against the business?

- Does the business have a positive employee culture? Does it engage in any charitable or environmental initiatives?

Capacity
- Is the business turning away new customers due to lack of equipment/ employees?

- Are the assets of the company (property, plant) strained or in a state of disrepair?

Capital
- Is the landscaping business carrying any debt? What is its debt ratio?

- What is the company's cash flow like over the last five years?

- What is the company's new account history? How much business is new vs. repeat?

Collateral
- Are any of the business' assets impaired in any way? Obsolete equipment, for instance?

Conditions
- Describe the market space the business occupies. Is it a leader? Are there many players?

- What defines dominance in this market? Cost? Economies of scale? Speed to market? Relationships with customers? Where does this business fall against the aforementioned metrics?

- Is the market for landscaping saturated? Are there opportunities for expanding the current customer base?

- What advertising and promotional activity has been done? How much does the business spend (as a percent of sales) on marketing its services?

10. You have inherited a start-up software company. How do you estimate market size? On which fronts do you anticipate problems?

Another great candidate for the five Cs. Here are some points adjusted for the unique dynamics of the start-up environment.

Character

- How would you evaluate the sincerity, honesty, and integrity of the owner of the business? Do others that they deal with (employees, suppliers, customers) value them as partners or are there character issues?

- Is there any legal action pending against the business?

- Does the mission of the startup make sense? Is its business concept sound?

- What is the timeline/progress of development, coding, testing, and production as originally conceived in the business plan? Does it make sense?

- What is the previous track record of each of the principals of the startup?

Capacity

- What is the plan for producing the product when the code is ready? Is it an option to outsource stamping, packaging and shipping?

Capital

- What is the makeup of the initial seed capital to start the business? Personal assets, small business loan, venture capital funds?

Visit the Vault Consulting Career Channel at **www.vault.com/consulting** — with
insider firm profiles, message boards, the Vault Consulting Job Board and more.

VAULT CAREER LIBRARY

95

• What is the debt structure like if it exists? Interest rates, due dates, rollover ability, secured assets, etc.?

Collateral

• Have any patents been applied for? What is their status?

• What has been done to protect the intellectual capital/property associated with the software design?

Conditions

• Describe the market space the business occupies. Why did the business come into inception?

• What defines dominance in this market? Cost? Economies of scale? Speed to market? Relationships with customers? Where does this business fall against the aforementioned metrics?

• Is the market for this type of product saturated? Is there a particular unfulfilled segment where this product fits, or will it be competing against other already established products?

• What is the advertising and promotional activity planned for this product?

11. Distribution Case

We have been engaged by a major entertainment company to assist them in building a distribution network for home video. They currently contract their distribution through other, more established entities, but the contracts with those companies are expiring, and it is unclear whether the new contracts contain favorable terms or not. There is still a chance that our client may continue to distribute their products through a third party. How would you assess whether to build a distribution network or continue the contracts with the third parties?

First of all, you need to ask your interviewer some basic questions:

• It makes sense to ask your interviewer about best practices – that is, what are other entertainment companies doing? What are the current costs? Does the company have the staff and resources to create its own distribution network?

- Of the major entertainment companies that produce video, do most distribute through their own proprietary supply chain or through third parties?

- What is the client's current cost of distribution through its contractual partner(s)?

- Has the client attempted to assess building its own distribution network before retaining us? If so, what were its findings?

- Does the client have a dedicated functional staff assigned to the project? If so, what functional areas do they represent?

After establishing some basic facts, it's time to get more detailed. Your interviewer may allude to certain avenues to discuss, or shut down others. If the interviewer confirms that, yes, the company does have enough current staff to handle setting up its own network, there's no call to delve deeper into the ramifications of reassigning personnel. Let's say that, through questioning, you've come to decide that staying with a third-party distributor makes the most sense. Now the question is – should the company stay with its current distributor, or choose a new one?

- Who are possible alternative partners? Who uses them?

- Could you characterize the relationship between the client's distribution partner and the client? Is there a possibility of retaliation on the part of the distribution partner if the client severs its ties to this party?

- How many weeks of supply are currently in the distribution partner's pipeline?

- How receptive are the client's accounts to changing distribution partners? Has a value proposition been created to show the client's accounts that a client-owned supply chain would be more efficient, valuable, etc. to the accounts?

- Does the client have any financial interest in the distribution partner that might have to be severed?

After answering these questions, make a recommendation.

12. A Powerful Case

You're a utilities company in a small town, and you're having trouble getting your customers to pay on time. What do you do?

First of all, you'll need to know what kind of company you are. Electric? Gas? Phone? Could it be that you are based in a small, rural area where customers turn to their wood-burning stoves for heat and cooking power instead of gas? Have your customers adopted cell phones en masse and are now neglecting their regular phone bills? You won't know until you pin down the problem – and then you can determine a solution for the company's woes.

Some questions you should ask:

- Where are we based?
- What is the composition of our customer base?
- What percentage of our customers are not paying on time?
- How much money do we lose from slow payers?
- How many of those slow payers never pay?
- Is there a certain segment of the population that is not paying?
- Is the area in a recession or slump that affects the ability of customers to pay their bills?
- How late are the payments of the slow payers?
- What do we currently do to motivate slow payers to pay their bills?
- Are there any government or state regulations that will affect our actions?
- At what point do we currently cut off slow payers? (Perhaps the company is so slow to do so that customers are taking advantage of the company. Or, if the town is small enough, it's possible that there are employees who refuse to cut off power to their friends and family.)

After you've determined the nature of the problem, you can make a recommendation on how to solve it. You may have more than one problem. Perhaps your small town is home to a university, and students move frequently and often neglect their last utilities bills. (Can you work out an arrangement with the university that denies diplomas or registration to students that neglect their bills? Should you start asking for second and third addresses and contact numbers? Perhaps requiring a deposit from students to turn on power?) At the same time, your company may need to start charging higher late fees to other customers who are simply taking advantage of the six months of forgiveness your utility gives.

13. Under Pressure

While most interviewers will be pleasant, there are some interviews that are seemingly designed to be stressful. Here's an actual example of how one "pressure case" started off:

Interviewer: Okay, what kind of case do you want?

Candidate: Huh?

Interviewer: We don't have much time. Give me a case.

Candidate: Um, market entry?

Interviewer: Okay. Truck leasing.

Candidate: What?

Interviewer: Truck leasing. Europe.

Candidate: Well, what countries in Europe are we targeting?

Interviewer: Wrong!

Candidate: (Taken aback) Who are our competitors?

Interviewer: Wrong.

Candidate: What kinds of trucks do we lease?

Interviewer: Wrong, wrong.

Candidate: I give up!

Interviewer: What is truck leasing?

It goes to show – you can never make assumptions in case interviews! Even if you think you understand truck leasing, or shrimp farming, or any other industry you're presented with – don't proceed without clarifying your suppositions with the interviewer.

A Written Case

Some cases are written and do not involve an interactive process between the interviewer and the candidate. Here's an example of an actual written case and a potential outline.

14. Widget Associates is a private equity placement firm with $3 billion in assets. They are primarily focused on the confluence of information and high technology and would like to utilize their assets in a manner consistent with this interest. Below, please describe your approach to the following:

- Assessing Widget Associates' strategic direction

- Evaluating its market interest and its potential for success

- Creating a value proposition that marries its strategic vision with marketplace dynamics

- Suggestions for initial placement of funds

Please be succinct with your answers. You may bullet point if you like. You have 30 minutes to complete the exercise.

The best way to approach written business case questions is to create a brief outline and then flesh out those points. Don't write too much, or in too much detail. This is a very easy mistake to make since you will be nervous and under time pressure. The art of answering written case interview questions successfully is to be succinct, logical, and speedy. An appropriate outline to use as a framework for this answer might be:

1) Strategic assessment

  (a) Industry assessment

  (b) Key members, market potential/forecast, volatility

  (c) Tools to use (Porter's Five Forces, BCG Matrix, etc.)

  (d) Widget's potential for a role in this industry

  (e) Risk assessment

2) Value Proposition

(a) Assessment of the value Widget brings to this industry

(b) Justification for injection of outside funds into this industry

3) Tactical effort

(a) Identification of a short list of primary targets

(b) Assess readiness of key players (management team, legal, financial, etc.)

(c) Evaluate all potential marketplace outcomes and validate against strategy

(d) Construction of workplan with milestones/deadlines and go/no decision points

This is probably an overly detailed outline, but you may choose to answer the question simply as above, with a little bit of detail attached to each sub-point. Remember that the interviewer isn't looking for The Great American Novel, or even flashes of what you perceive as wit. Just include the actions you would take to assess, evaluate, analyze, and recommend action for the situation.

The Financial Case Interview

Case interviews aren't just for consultants any more. Many investment banks give questions that could, under other circumstances, be called case interviews – they often involve both strategy and quantitative know-how. Consulting firms often use similar cases. Here are a few such questions.

15. What is a company that you follow closely? Is it a good investment?

Tell your interviewer you would look at various criteria to determine if it's a worthwhile investment, including:

- **Earnings growth:** Determine how fast the company's earnings are expected to grow, looking at the following factors (among others): the company's historic growth rate; earnings growth rates of other companies in the industry; growth rate of the market the company services; analyst estimates; and perhaps building your own financial model in Excel to test various assumptions.

- **Industry analysis:** Evaluate the industry the company is in to determine whether this is an attractive industry in which to invest. Look at factors including: how rapidly the industry is growing; whether the industry is consolidating; how intense the competition is among competitors; whether market players have pricing power; and whether products are considered commodities.

- **Competitive advantages:** Evaluate whether the company has any competitive advantages over its competition, such as patents, exclusive contracts, a differentiated product, brand equity, a lower cost structure, or superior management.

- **Valuation:** Given its prospects, is the company a good value? You would compare the company's expected earnings growth to various valuation measures, like price-to-earnings ratio, price-to-sales ratio, and price-to-book-value. You would also compare these valuation measures to other companies in the industry to determine whether the company is relatively expensive or relatively affordable.

- **Portfolio considerations:** Finally, you would want to determine whether an investment in the company fits well with your overall portfolio and objectives. You would want to ask questions like: Does the company help diversify risk in your portfolio? Does the company meet your portfolio's risk profile?

16. You represent a major food manufacturer. You have been asked to assess the potential acquisition of a premium priced flour company based in the Southeast. The asking price is $130 million. The company's profit after tax this year is $11.2 million. You have audited financial information, and you can do interviews.

First, assess whether the asking price of $130 million is in the ballpark of reason, and determine what the target's value is to your client.

Calculate the baseline value – the value of the company with constant margins and zero growth. The value of the company (or net present value) = cash flow/ discount rate. (Cash Flow = Net Income – Capital Expenditures + Depreciation +/- Changes in Working Capital)

At zero growth, Cap X should equal depreciation, and the working capital will be stable. Therefore, Cash Flow = Net Operating Profit after Tax.

Cash Flow divided by the discount rate is the net present value (Let's say the discount rate is 0.10. if your interviewer asks, tell him you would calculate the discount rate using the Capital Asset Pricing Model). Let's say Cash Flow divided by the discount rate is $112 million. Assuming $8 million in goodwill tax write-offs, the total baseline value is $120.

What is the market position of the flour company? Let's say your interviewer gives you this chart:

Flour Share
Target's 3-State Market Area

Visit the Vault Consulting Career Channel at www.vault.com/consulting — with
insider firm profiles, message boards, the Vault Consulting Job Board and more.
VAULT CAREER
LIBRARY
103

Now you must ask your interviewer questions to supplement your knowledge about the flour company.

You: Will price increases be sustainable? How much will prices increase per year? How modern are the facilities?

Interviewer: Price increases have been seen every year, and prices will probably continue to rise over the next five years, 2 to 3 percent per year.

You: Will further expansion into other markets be possible? What is the firm's share in non-core markets?

Interviewer: Less than 2 percent. While the firm has expanded into non-core markets, advertising and marketing costs are very high. Share gains are possible but slowly and at a lower margin than existing businesses.

What are the possible synergies with the food manufacturer? Sketch out a chart:

Potential Synergy	NPV Impact ($M)	Probability	NPV Impact x Probability ($M)
Economies of scale in purchasing	20.0	60%	12.0
Leverage distribution capabilities in outlying markets	12.0	70%	8.4
Leverage know-how to improve revenue realization for by-product	14.0	70%	9.8
Provide learning experience in value-added consumer products	?	?	?
		Total	30.2

The baseline value is $120 million. While it is uncertain how much upside there will be in market expansion, synergies are likely to be at least $30 million.

From this you can ascertain:

The flour business is mature, but secure. Its volume declines are set off by price increases. Its brand position should allow a price premium. The flour business is a good buy.

Additional Practice Questions

17. You have been appointed the manager of a rental car company. How do you measure its efficiency?

This case question is a good candidate for the Value Chain approach.

- What are your expenses (cars, insurance, rental of car office, advertising)?

- What is your average rental time period? (On average how long is a car checked out?)

- How fast is a vehicle turned around (from drop-off to back on the line)? What is the industry average for this turnaround?

- What percentage of your fleet is down for repairs on average? How does this compare to the industry?

- What percentage of your employees calls in sick every day on average? How does this compare to the industry?

- Does the business exhibit any seasonality (for example, are you located near a ski resort that sees business boom in the winter)? How do you account for these effects?

Another way to look at this question is to use a real-life "out-of-the-box" approach. Why not simply look out on the lot and see how many cars are rented out at any given time, and what kind they are – and do this over a period of time in different locations? This kind of real-world approach will win points with consultants, who actually have to drive around and look at parking lots at 4 a.m. (and other such hijinx) more often than they would probably like.

18. Our client has engaged us to assist them in reorganizing their sales force. They want to cut $50 million in costs from this area over the next two years.

This is an organizational change question. What is especially important here is to balance the financial realities of the situation against the organizational impact of head count reduction, the introduction of new technologies, etc. Questions that would help focus this situation include:

- What is the primary business for this client?

- What is the timeline for the reorganization process?

- What is the early estimate of how many people could be involved?

- What is the scope of change? Does it include downsizing, the introduction of technologies, closing/selling-off of locations, reengineering business processes?

- What is the early assessment of the organizational climate for change? Are they receptive or resistant? What are the reasons for resistance if any?

- Can you describe any dynamics unique to this client's business that put the success of the project at risk?

- What are the major risk factors surrounding this project?

- What are the measurements of success for this project?

19. Your client is trying to decide whether or not to invest in a helicopter company. You have been asked to assess the long-term attractiveness of the helicopter market.

Since this case is primarily asking for an industry analysis (is this an attractive industry?), Porter's Five Forces is one framework useful in formulating your recommendation.

20. A large health care company has hired you to determine a strategy for improving profitability through growth. The company hopes to reach its goal in three years. What do you advise?

Note that your interviewer will often impose deadlines and other "constraints" that represent the wishes of the client (for example, the client wants to reach its goal within six months; the company wants to reach its goal without spending more than $5 million; etc.). You should not necessarily be constrained by the company's hoped-for timelines or budget constraints, unless your interviewer tells you otherwise. In this case, you should question whether three years is a realistic or even optimal timeline. Your job is to recommend the best course of action, including an optimal timeline, not to take your client's wishes as representing the best course of action.

21. Our client, ABC Airlines, is losing money. Why?

Remember to consider the firm's actions as well as external market forces such as the competitive environment. Questions include asking whether other airlines are losing money, or suffering drops in profits. If so, why? Causes might range from a rise in the cost of fuel, to the need to replace most of ABC's fleet due to stringent new government regulations, to a general slump in the economy that reduces the number of tourists and causes business customers to tighten their belts.

22. You are head of a large American corporation. Your company must build a new paper plant. You must decide which country to build the plant in. What factors would you consider?

Analyze your supply chain. Where do you incur your costs? If your paper plant is highly automated, it might make more sense to build it in America or another developed country where you have access to skilled labor. If, on the other hand, your paper plant requires thousands of employees, you may want to consider a country or region of America where the cost of labor is lower.

23. Your client is a major airline that wants to reduce the amount of money it spends per passenger on food service, ticketing, and baggage handling. What would you advise?

Benchmarking is one good starting point for this type of case. You would certainly want to know (or at least be able to estimate) how much other airlines spend on each passenger for food service, ticketing, and baggage handling. Are your client's costs in each of these areas high or low for the industry?

You would also want to examine "best practices": which airlines have the lowest costs in each of the three areas of food service, ticketing, and baggage handling? What are they doing right, and how can we emulate it? (Remember that best practices for a particular process may be found outside the airline industry. For example, how do passenger railroads or cruise ships ticket their passengers? Are companies in that industry doing anything particularly well that may apply to the airline business?)

24. A multi-billion dollar consumer brand product manufacturer is considering introducing its flagship brand into Asia. What would you advise?

This is an example of a broad question where you must first assess the situation in more detail. A series of "helicoptering" questions:

- Why has the company engaged our services?

- What are the risk factors associated with this project?

- What is the timing for our involvement with this client and this project?

- What is the nature of the client's business? What is their flagship brand?

- What business unit within the organization has engaged us?

You should have more information about the nature of the project after these questions. From here, you can pursue a more specific series of questions. Let's say that in response to your questions, you learn that the project involves a software package selection for automating trade promotions activity in preparation for entry into Asia. (Now you see why it's so important to ask questions.) The next set of questions you should ask would be drilldowns – teasing out the finer points – on the information you've just gathered. For example:

- Have any vendors been identified for the selection? If so, whom?

- What is the timeframe for the package selection?

- What client staff will be participating in the project? What are their roles in the organization?

- What experience does the firm have with similar engagements/industries? Can we draw upon that experience for this engagement? Why or why not?

- Has a workplan been developed for this project? What is an overview of this plan?

- What are the measures that have been established to evaluate the success of this selection?

And Try These for More Practice

25. **Eastern Newspapers is a large newspaper chain that is considering diversifying into non-newspaper media assets and is a potential client for our firm's M&A group. How would you go about advising this client? What information would you want to gather before you meet with the client?**

26. **JerseyWeb is a small Internet access provider with $20 million in annual revenues. JerseyWeb is considering acquiring another small Internet access provider in nearby Connecticut. What would you advise JerseyWeb to do?**

27. **A major ski resort currently forbids snowboarding, but is considering allowing the sport. What should it consider before allowing or disallowing snowboarding?**

28. The maple syrup market has four main competitors. The market share and price per unit are as follows.

Absolute Syrup share 42 percent   price per unit $5.00

Beastly Syrup   share 27 percent   price per unit $4.10

Catchall Syrup share 16 percent   price per unit $3.50

Delight Syrup   share 15 percent   price per unit $3.55

What kind of market is this?

29. You are Britney Spears. You are afraid that MP3s will hurt sales of your music. What should you do?

INTERACTIVE CASES

A Fit Interview in Disguise

You've memorized the frameworks and you've walked through the practice cases. Congratulations! You've aced the analysis half of case interview preparation. Now it's time to build on your skills and add the second half of your preparation: delivery.

It is one thing to tear apart a business problem in the privacy of your own space. But it is an entirely different endeavor to walk through that analysis out loud for a complete stranger – someone who is prepared to challenge your thoughts and be even a bit antagonistic. How many of us have tried to explain a solution to someone else and stumbled on words, stuttered, threw in a few too many um's, or had to retrace our steps after losing our place? Poor presentation in an interview can sink you – consultants are assessing your poise as much as your intellect.

In fact, smart candidates realize that the case interview is an audition. The interviewer is getting a snapshot of what it would be like to work with you. It's not just about what's going on upstairs. How good are you at communicating your logic? How would clients perceive you? What would you be like to work with on a team? It is just as important to practice the actual vocal delivery of the analysis as it is to be able to think through the analysis itself.

We know of a handful of people who walked right into their first case interview and nailed it. But for most of us, the case interview can be a tougher communication proposition than public speaking. The better prepared you are to walk through your thinking aloud and explain your analysis in clear, succinct sentences, the better you will do at the real thing.

How to Use the Interactive Cases

The good news is, you can crack this part of the case, too. The best way to practice your poise is to practice with someone else. That's where these interactive case exercises come in.

The idea of our interactive case exercises is to simulate the case interview environment as closely as possible. (Remember, the case interview is designed to simulate the actual consulting environment – the interviewer is your client and may provide certain background data necessary to solve the problem, but you may have to make estimates and assumptions, and you will have to provide the approach.)

The following set of cases is designed for two people to practice with each other. Have one person play the interviewer and the other person be the interviewee. The interviewer should read through the case beforehand, understand the analysis, and be prepared to guide the interviewee through the case. Make sure the interviewee hasn't read through the case ahead of time. (If you plan to use these cases yourself, STOP and find someone to practice with you!)

How To Run an Interactive Case Exercise

As you'll see, each of these cases has five sections.

• **Context** – Initial setup for the case.

• **Question** – What the interviewee needs to answer in solving the case.

• **Background data** – Additional information that the interviewer will reveal to the interviewee as he or she is asked for it.

• **Suggested approach** – One possible solution to the case.

• **Study notes** – A few key tips for solving the case.

To run one of these case interviews, the designated interviewer should read and understand the entire case exercise ahead of time. He or she should be prepared to answer questions from the interviewee based on the case.

To begin the practice session, the interviewer should read the context and question sections directly to the interviewee. The interviewee should then ask questions of the interviewer about the facts of the case, with the interviewer revealing information from the background data section as necessary.

If you're the interviewer, you must analyze not just the answers the interviewee gives, but the logic behind them. If the interviewee makes an assumption or states a fact without giving logical reasons for her assumption, ask "Why do you think that?" or "Where are you going with your analysis?"

It's the interviewer's responsibility to nudge things along if they've reached an impasse. If the interviewee is completely stuck, offer a data point from the background data provided or assist the interviewee in reaching the next logical step in the analysis.

At the end of the data section, you'll find a follow-up question.   The interviewer should pose this question after the interviewee has answered the main question. This happens in real cases when the interviewee has done well; it's designed to push the interviewee even further and to simulate real engagements, when things routinely come up at the last minute.

Scoring the case

After the case, the interviewer should give the interviewee balanced feedback on his or her performance and go over the study notes. For example, you can score the interviewer's performance as follows:

a) **Presentation** – Shook hands, smiled, was well-dressed, and displayed solid manners and business etiquette throughout. Maintained eye contact throughout the interview. (10 points)

b) **Communication** – Relayed thoughts and ideas to interviewer clearly and succinctly. Explained thought processes in sufficient detail for the interviewer. (30 points)

c) **Quantitative Skills** – Showed good facility with numbers, including guesstimates (15 points)

d) **Problem Solving** – Followed a logical, thorough, well-connected path of reasoning to solve the answer. Laid out a road map upfront and continued to think out loud. Used a framework if appropriate. Showed the ability to be flexible and change directions if the interviewer wanted to guide the case a different way. (30 points)

e) **Summary** – Wrapped up the case for the interviewer, bringing together the pieces of the puzzle and offering thoughtful recommendations and follow-up insights. (10)

f) **Questions** – Asked the interviewer two or three thoughtful questions specific to the interviewer's firm. (5 points)

Tips for the Case

Here are a few pointers to make sure you get the most out of the interactive case exercises.

For the interviewer

If you are the interviewer, be realistic. Real consulting interviewers are, on average, businesslike yet fully intending to help you crack the case. Don't be overly willing to volunteer the background information without being asked, but if the interviewee asks for a piece of information that is listed, go ahead and reveal it. If the interviewee comes up with some brilliant point that is not covered in your materials, acknowledge that a good point has been made, and then steer the conversation back to the case at hand.

Simulate the actual case interview format

If you really want to simulate a case interview, don't start with the case solving right away. Here is the typical format for a case interview:

1) Direct fit questions: (5-10 minutes)
2) Case question (15-20 minutes)
3) Questions for the interviewer (3-5 minutes)

Note that case interviews often start with a handful of fit interview questions, and almost all of the time they will fall in some form of three basic questions. These are "Why do you want to be a consultant?" "Why do you want to work for this firm?" and "Why should we hire you?" The interviewee should have quick, thorough answers to these questions ready. The interviewee should also have some basic questions ready for the interviewee about "his" firm.

For the interviewee

If you are the interviewee, bring your leather notepad and favorite pen. Review the frameworks in this guide and apply them judiciously. Don't forget to take notes while the interviewer is speaking, and nod and paraphrase to demonstrate good listening. Above all, don't forget to answer the question – or at least to understand what the question is!

Practice communicating in a succinct, clear, engaging manager. For example, lay out your approach ahead of time for the interviewer. When you are transitioning to the next step of your analysis, signal that fact clearly. "That seems to cover revenues. Let's move onto costs next. I think the variable costs could be the most important part, so let's start there." If your interviewer wants you to spend more time on a part of your analysis, this will give him the chance to communicate this to you.

You never know what kind of personality your interviewer will have, and you don't want to get used to a certain case giver's style. Moreover, as mock interviewers, we might tend to be a little more forgiving of our friends. Try practicing with folks you don't know very well but are willing to help you. These include current consultants, alumni of your school, career services employees, or fellow students.

If you run out of interactive cases, feel free to take previous cases in this book and convert them into the interactive case format. You can also make up cases on your own. Take them from previous work experiences, classroom case studies, or business ideas you've been drumming up in your head.

Sample Interactive Cases

1. Magazine Publishing Company

Your client, MediaCo, is a publishing company that creates and delivers a magazine with national distribution. Currently, it has two operating plants: one in upstate New York, and one in Oregon. It is considering shutting down one of the plants in order to save costs.

Question: What should MediaCo do?

Background data

• Both plants are at equal capacity.

• Each plant has identical costs of production at 75 cents per magazine.

- Paper: 40 cents/magazine

- Ink: 35 cents/magazine

• Assume there are no other costs of production.

• MediaCo could benefit from economies of scale of production if it were to produce from just one plant. This would result in a 20% savings in the inking process but no savings in the paper process.

- MediaCo delivers its magazines from its plants to regional post offices at the cost of 35 cents per magazine. This cost is the same for each plant.

- The costs of distribution would change if MediaCo had just one operational plant.

  - Delivery would cost 37 cents per magazine if MediaCo were to deliver only from the New York plant.

  - Delivery would cost 43 cents per magazine if MediaCo were to deliver only from the Oregon plant.

- There are no additional costs besides those of production and distribution. There are no additional fixed costs of production and distribution.

- Either plant could produce the entire capacity without additional costs.

- There are no international subscriptions, and the company has no plan to seek any.

Suggested approach

A cost-benefit framework will work well for this case. In terms of benefits, there are three possible scenarios (keep both plants, shut down New York, or shut down Oregon), and we have enough information to assess the impact upon margins in each. In terms of costs, we can determine possible negative impacts to each scenario.

Let's analyze the two major cost buckets: production and distribution.

Production – If the company were to produce from a single plant, it would reduce its inking costs from 35 cents to 28 cents, so the overall cost would decrease from 75 cents to 68 cents per magazine. This cost savings would occur if either plant were shut down.

Distribution – We now know that it is more expensive to deliver out of just one plant (the case giver might push the receiver to explain why). Moreover, because it costs more to deliver from Oregon, we can infer that most of the readership is in the Eastern U.S.

We can now work out the per magazine costs under each scenario:

Keep both plants – Total cost per magazine is $0.75 + $0.35 = $1.10
Shut down Oregon – Total cost per magazine is $0.68 + $0.37 = $1.05
Shut down New York – Total cost per magazine is $0.68 + $0.43 = $1.11

Therefore, it saves MediaCo the most money to shut down Oregon and run the magazine entirely out of the New York plant. The interviewee should recommend this solution.

Follow-up

Ask the interviewee to address possible downsides to shutting down one of the plants. These include the following:

• **Layoffs** – It is likely that MediaCo would have to reduce headcount. This might create bad publicity and general ill will.

• **Possible shutdown costs** – MediaCo should investigate any additional costs it might incur if it were to shut down a plant. Does it need to pay a fee to break a lease? What long-term overhead contracts does it have?

• **Shortsighted decision-making** – Costs are never constant and could change after any period of time. Are current costs highly indicative of future costs?

Finally, the interviewee could be asked to suggest alternatives to the shutdown proposal. Possibilities include:

• Close the Oregon plant briefly as a test. This retains the "real option" to reopen it at a later date.

• If it is cost-effective, create a new plant in between Oregon and New York to alleviate the discrepancy in distribution costs and still achieve the economies of scale in production. MediaCo might also look into buying a plant from a competitor, or looking abroad to build or buy a plant if it is cheaper there.

2. Broadband Software Company

Your client, SoftCo, is a startup software firm. They have built a cutting-edge software package for cable broadband companies. However, they are technologists without much business knowledge, and they have called you in to help them understand the economics of their industry.

Question: How attractive is the cable broadband software industry? What should SoftCo do?

Background data

• Cable broadband software providers offer packages that help with any aspect of maintaining a cable offering to customers, including start-up procedure and administration.

• SoftCo makes provisioning software, which helps cable operators to install and maintain high-speed Internet cable service for end customers.

• Cable broadband software providers offer packages that help with any aspect of maintaining a cable offering to customers. This might include provisioning, billing, configuration, speed enhancements, or customer care packages.

• The main costs of software development are labor and technology (such as hardware and licensing). It is quite easy to find computer programmers and computer software. Development software is expensive but not unreasonable.

• It is very important for the software to reflect actual business flows in the cable operator's provisioning business. SoftCo spent many hours interviewing cable operators to understand how they install, maintain, and provide customer service.

• Provisioning services require some sort of software. Hardware could theoretically be manually configured, but with millions of subscribers across the United States, this isn't feasible.

• Cable operators are large companies that tend to prefer outsourcing provisioning software development. They like to choose intuitive, easy-to-learn packages that are scalable and that can handle their large capacity. Most cable operators have an enormous customer base.

• There are currently 23 players in the cable broadband software space. 12 of them currently make a provisioning product. The rest make software in the cable broadband space for related aspects, such as billing.

• The market size is rather large and growing at a steady 4% a year, post-Internet boom.

• No one player in any aspect of provisioning (or cable broadband) has more than 10% market share.

• Use of new cable broadband software requires two weeks of training per person, on average.

Suggested approach

The question calls for an industry assessment, and Porter's Five Forces is usually the best framework for this type of question. The background information contains all of the information necessary to create a high-level yet comprehensive assessment of the cable broadband space; thorough questions from the interviewee will result in a successful analysis.

Lay out a structure (Porter's) at the beginning of the case that lets the interviewer know what information you think you need to answer the question

Follow that structure and communicate to the interviewer when you transition from one part of the structure to another. Consider including a very brief summary of where you are and what you've learned in your transitions

Ask probing, open questions to gather the necessary information and clarify if necessary

At the end, summarize your findings, synthesize the "so-what" insights, and formulate a conclusion, and offer a recommendation

Using Porter's Five Forces, the industry can be analyzed as follows:

• Potential entrants – Entry barriers are fairly low in most software industries. This one, with low cost of labor and materials, is no exception. The interviewee might suggest that cable expertise is necessary, and this is true, but the interviewer should suggest that cable know-how is not difficult to acquire.

• Buyer power – Buyer power is tremendous. The products are probably not highly differentiated (since there are not many different features to offer), and the fixed cost of changing software packages is low at two weeks of training.

• Supplier power – This is probably low, as it is not difficult to find software programmers and development platforms

• Threat of substitutes – There is no real substitute for this product. Hardware isn't a feasible alternative.

• Competition – We would expect competition to be fierce. Indeed, there are 23 players in the arena, with 12 direct competitors, and it is highly likely that the other 11 players would offer provisioning as a natural fit.

The interviewee should wrap up his overview of the industry with the following summary:

• The industry is probably highly fragmented, with lots of small players. It will likely get worse.

• Competition is intense, and with the possibility of some of the remaining 11 players entering the market, it could get even more competitive.

• We might expect the industry to have largely similar products, differing mostly in look and feel.

• With fierce price competition, profit margins would be low.

The interviewee should conclude that the industry is not attractive.

Follow-up question

What options does SoftCo have? The interviewee could suggest some options for the client:

• Seek to be acquired by a large cable operator

• Seek to merge with one or more of the competition to increase scale and market share and therefore increase attractiveness to cable operators. Another option would be a merger with a technology software provider who provides a related product (DSL provisioning, cable TV).

• Exit the industry

Study notes

The key takeaway from this case is to choose an appropriate framework. Remember that for industry analysis, nothing beats Porter's Five Forces. You would not be using Porter's Five Forces if the question had prompted you to examine a particular company internally; Porter's is a checklist that is strictly external to the firm. Be careful not to say something like, "I will be using Porter's Five Forces for this case," as such a statement suggests that you are tied more to a framework and less to original analytical thinking.

Remember to wrap up your framework with a summary, especially in a data-heavy case like this one. Bring it all together at the end with a concise, hard-hitting, bottom-line flourish.

3. Refrigerator manufacturer

Your client, FreezeCo, is one of the leading manufacturers of refrigerators. FreezeCo has noticed its profits declining in the recent past.

Question: Why are profits declining? What can FreezeCo do?

Background Data

- Sales volume has been flat over time.

- Market prices have not changed during the period in question.

- The industry is led by four major players, including FreezeCo. However, none of the players have created any significant new products or started any aggressive marketing campaigns. As a result, market share has remained relatively stable.

- FreezeCo sells directly to its customers, mostly residential management companies. This customer market has been quite stable over the last few years, though there has been a trend towards buying as opposed to rentals.

- FreezeCo has three kinds of costs: labor, materials, and overhead. Overall overhead has not unchanged, but overall labor and material costs have increased.

- Manufacturing costs are highly variable. As a result, there are no economies of scale of production.

- Variable costs per refrigerator have not changed.

- FreezeCo builds and sells two different kinds of refrigerators, a larger model and a smaller model. Recently, FreezeCo's sales department has noticed an increase in the number of larger models being sold.

- Margins are higher for the smaller model than they are for the larger model.

Suggested approach

The interviewee could use either the Four C's or the cost-benefit framework to crack this case. Here is an example of how the interviewee might discuss the Four C's:

- **Customers** – The customer base seems to be stable overall, as sales volume has been flat. However, it seems that the market for FreezeCo products has changed. Customers are more interested in buying the larger refrigerator.

As it turns out, people who buy homes prefer the larger model, and the residential management companies who are FreezeCo's primary customers are changing their purchase patterns from FreezeCo accordingly.

- **Competition** – The background information indicates that competition really isn't a factor in FreezeCo's declining profits. Market share has been constant.

- **Cost** – FreezeCo's cost position hasn't changed. However, they are selling more of the larger refrigerators, each of which requires more labor and materials than the smaller refrigerators.

- **Capabilities** – The key point here is the production system. Since FreezeCo has no economies of scale of production, FreezeCo's overall costs are increasing from the shift in product mix.

The interviewee should conclude that the product mix is shifting from smaller refrigerators to larger refrigerators. Because margins are lower for the larger refrigerators, FreezeCo profits have fallen.

Possible recommendations include the following:

- Overhaul the production system – The fact that FreezeCo can't achieve economies of scale is a problem. FreezeCo should investigate new production systems that would allow for economies of scale of production. This would require research and an ROI calculation. The disadvantage is that this is likely to be a long-term solution.

- Address sourcing – Could FreezeCo achieve additional economies of scale in purchasing its materials? Perhaps it could renegotiate its contracts with its suppliers, given the shift in market demand, to obtain cheaper inputs based on volume purchasing.

Additional recommendations might include the following:

- Increase prices – If buyers are brand loyal and there is flexibility within the contracts, FreezeCo could consider increasing its prices slightly for the larger model. It might justify the slight price increase by adding a feature or releasing an "updated" version of the same model.

- Develop a new product – Since consumers increasingly want larger refrigerators, FreezeCo could attempt to develop a new large model that could garner a substantially higher price and generate higher margins.

- Ride it out – If the market shift is temporary, FreezeCo could choose to not change its production system. While this is a risky strategy, it should be addressed nonetheless.

Study notes

Using frameworks like the Four C's is a great way to make sure you've covered all bases. However, your interviewer might not be interested in hearing yet another recitation of those dreaded C-words. Introduce your framework in a way that is natural for you. For example, you might disguise the Four C's framework as follows: "First, I'd like to look externally, or outside of the firm. The key areas here would be competition and customer base. After that, I'd like to look internally at the firm, focusing on two areas: costs and the firm's resources." In other words, what framework you use doesn't matter, as long as you structure your thinking.

4. Drug Insurance

Your client, DrugCo, is a United States drug manufacturer. It has recently invented a drug that treats Alzheimer's Disease. The drug comes in the form of an oral tablet that, if taken daily, significantly reduces the chance of Alzheimer's. The drug has no side effects whatsoever.

A major component of the pharmaceutical industry in the United States is insurance. Assume, for this case, that insurance companies currently provide complete coverage for the medical bills of Alzheimer's patients. As much as insurance companies are interested in preventing Alzheimer's, they are concerned that covering the drug will be more expensive to them than covering the current medical costs of Alzheimer's.

Question: DrugCo is considering pricing the drug at $30 a month. Are insurance companies likely to provide coverage for this drug?

Background data

- The product is completely unique. There are no viable substitutes or competitors on the horizon.

- The drug is FDA-approved.

- The drug is available through prescription through doctors.

- Medical bills for Alzheimer's average $60,000. This is currently fully covered by insurance companies. Insurance companies are unlikely to want to insure a treatment more expensive that this.

- The potential customers are Americans aged 50 and older who are considered "high risk" for Alzheimer's.

- 40% of the US population over 50 is considered high risk.

- In the past, 1/6 of all high risk Americans have had Alzheimer's by age 70.

- 20% of the US population is over 50.

(Note: this data is fictitious and was created solely for instructional purposes.)

Suggested approach

The goal of the case is to determine a price point at which an insurance company would be indifferent between covering the drug prescription and covering the expected medical costs of a high-risk individual. This requires the case interviewee to size the number of high-risk individuals in the US, and the interviewer should guide the interviewee in the direction of this calculation. Many case interviews, particularly those regarding new product entry, require the candidate to do a back-of-the-envelope market sizing as a part of the analysis (though not the end goal). This case is a good example. This is also a great opportunity to walk through sizing calculations out loud!

In this case, the assumptions for percentages are given, but the interviewer might also push the interviewee to make assumptions for the percentages above as part of the sizing. As long as the assumptions are clearly stated, the interviewee can make any assumptions necessary.

Here is the market sizing for high-risk individuals, given the assumptions above:

- Assume there are 300 million persons in the United States.

- We know that 20% are over 50. So, there are 60 million Americans who are 50 and older.

- We know that 40% of these are considered high risk. Therefore, there are 24 million high-risk individuals.

- Finally, we know that 1/6 of all high risk individuals have had Alzheimer's by age 70, so we would expect that 4 million would have Alzheimer's by age 70.

The interviewee can now walk through the calculations to compare current Alzheimer's coverage for patients aged 70 years versus drug coverage for high-risk patients from age 50 to age 70.

Current

• Currently, the insurance company expects to pay for all Alzheimer's patients. We expect that 4 million will become Alzheimer's patients. At $60,000 per patient, insurance companies would expect to pay a total of $240 billion.

• The interviewee should consider the time value of money. Discounting 20 years, assuming a discount rate of 10%, we calculate $39.24 billion. (The interviewer could suggest that the 10%, 20-yr discount factor is 1/6 to make things simple, and the interviewee would arrive at a total cost of $40 billion.)

New Drug

• There are 24 million individuals, and at $30 a month for 20 years, the total cost would be 24 million x $30/month x 12 months/year x 20 years = $172.80 billion. Assuming a discount rate of 10% for this 20-year perpetuity, we conclude that the drug coverage would cost $80.91 billion in today's dollars. (The discount factor here is $1/6$).

Given the current prices, insurance is unlikely to cover the drug.

Follow-up question

Given this information, how should DrugCo price the drug? The interviewee has enough information to figure this out.

• We don't want to exceed total cost of $40 billion in today's dollars, or $80 billion (backing out the discount factor of $1/6$) over 20 years. This equates to $4 billion a year.

• Dividing this by 24 million people, we have $166 per person per year, or roughly $14 dollars a month per person.

Therefore, DrugCo should price the drug at less than $14 per month per person. Depending on DrugCo's cost structure, it might want to even go significantly lower to create incentives for insurance companies to cover the drug.

Study notes

While the goal of this case is specifically to understand if an insurance company would cover the drug at $30 per month, a good consultant (interviewee) will also always proactively consider broader implications that may be outside the scope of the specific query. An excellent way to wrap up this case would be to raise the issue of public policy. Would insurance companies be forced to cover the drug? So would DrugCo be compelled to make the drug affordable through governmental action? How would regulatory edicts, buyer/supplier power, and public pressure combine to affect what portion of the drug cost is absorbed by insurance companies, DrugCo, and consumers? Finally, how much of the cost could be covered through overseas sales?

5. Brokerage Profitability

Your client, Futures Limited, is a commodity and financial futures brokerage serving institutional investors. Net income has declined over the past five years, and the company is now in danger of not meeting the financial hurdles that its parent, Futures Incorporated, has established for it.

Question: Why is Futures Limited having profitability problems?

Background data

• Futures Limited brokers buy and sell orders for commodity futures (e.g. wheat, oil, sugar) and financial futures (e.g. S&P500 future, interest rate futures).

• The company has several revenue sources:

    – Execution of orders on exchanges

    – Clearing (back-office processing of trades)

    – Net interest income from customer margin deposits

• A customer can choose to execute and/or clear trades with a given broker.

• One order can be for any specified number of contracts.

• A customer is charged a commission per contract that is inversely tied to the number of contracts in the order (the "lot size"):

    – 500-lot order: 50 cents per contract

    – 200-lot order: 75 cents per contract

  – 100-lot order: $1 per contract

  – 50-lot order: $1.50 per contract

  – 10-lot order: $5 per contract

- Processing an order involves a fixed amount of work, independent of the lot size.

- Total order volume is unchanged.

- The average number of contracts per order has declined from 100 to 62 over the past five years.

- The average order size across the institutional derivatives brokerage industry is estimated to be 120 contracts.

- The Federal Reserve Board has been reducing interest rates to battle a recessionary economy; when interest rates go down, absolute spreads are squeezed as well.

- Many derivatives exchanges have converted to electronic – as opposed to "open outcry" – trading in recent years.

- Annual capital investment has been at a historical high for the company in each of the last five years. The company has invested in a new back-office processing system, new order entry software, and system upgrades to ensure connectivity to global derivatives exchanges.

- Futures Limited's top five customers have closed their accounts in the last five years. Those customers tended to place 500-lot orders.

- The company's sales force has brought on 10 new customers over the last five years, but these customers tend to trade 75 contracts at a time. All other customers have maintained a constant average order size over the period.

Suggested approach

This is a straightforward profit analysis. The interviewee will want to highlight all of the possible factors that could influence profit levels:

- **Revenue** – Has total revenue decreased? Has the company reduced prices? Has order volume, contract volume or number of customers dwindled? Have interest rate spreads narrowed? Has the mix of types of orders changed?

- **Fixed costs** – Has overhead increased?

- **Variable costs** – Has the cost of processing a trade increased?

- **Capital investment** – Have significant new investments been made? Has depreciation increased?

- **Extraordinary items** – Have there been any one-time charges below the operating line?

- **Taxes** – Has the company's tax liability changed?

Given the interviewer's answers to these questions, we now know that there are three drivers of lower profit in Futures Limited:

- **Narrowing interest spreads**: This revenue stream is no longer contributing as much to the top line.

- **Higher capital costs**: Due to the migration to electronic trading, Futures Ltd. has had to spend more and more on technology in recent years.

- **Declining order size**: Since processing costs are incurred per order, total variable costs have remained constant. A key insight is that Futures Limited's pricing schedule reflects a total price per order that declines as the lot size decreases. (500-lot order @ 50 cents/contract = $250/order; 10-lot order @ $5/contract = $50/order) Total execution and clearing revenue has decreased as a result of the declining order size. Thus, operating margins are lower.

We now understand the reason for narrowing interest spreads and higher capital costs. Let's uncover the root cause of the declining order size. First, the interviewee needs to determine if the problem is internal to the firm, or industry-wide.

- Is the industry as a whole seeing declining order sizes?

- Is order size declining for all of Futures Ltd.'s customers?

- Can we look at data on how average order size has changed across different portions of Futures Limited's customer base?

We can conclude that Futures Limited had a highly concentrated revenue base five years ago. The company has since seen attrition among its top customers, who tended to trade large lots. It has replaced those customers with new customers who trade with similar frequency, but in smaller lot sizes.

Follow-up question

The interviewee could be asked to suggest initiatives to reverse the company's profit trend. These include:

• Revise the pricing schedule to reflect a constant price per order, independent of lot size.

• Seek new customers who have a need to trade large lots frequently.

• Incentivize customer behavior that will support profitability – institute minimum trading activity levels with fees for falling short.

• Review alternatives for more automated (cheaper) processing of small orders.

• Evaluate outsourcing and partnering alternatives to future large-scale capital investment in technology and trading systems.

• Pre-empt any additional attrition by identifying why top customers left and improving problematic aspects of the customer experience.

• Expanding into new, higher-margin service lines.

Note that each of these alternatives involves a different implementation timeframe. The interviewee could recommend a staged series of initiatives, beginning with suggestions for realizing the most immediate bottom-line improvement.

Study notes

Sometimes a case interview will discuss an industry that is unfamiliar to most interviewees. The interviewer wants to test your ability to quickly grasp the key issues at hand and not become distracted or confused by the technology or process that the hypothetical company employs. In this case, the fact that the company is a futures brokerage (as opposed to a more familiar stock brokerage) is not central to the profitability question.

6. Bridge Feasibility Study

Your client, DevCo, is an international infrastructure developer. DevCo specializes in building and operating roads and bridges, recovering its investment through toll charges. It typically enters a new country by bidding on and winning a concession from the government – which, in general, is simply the right for a party build and operate infrastructure for a set period of time. Currently, it is submitting a competitive bid to build a new toll bridge over a river in Argentina to connect two cities. The government requests bids in terms of a toll rate charged per vehicle.

Question: How would you go about determining what toll rate to bid?

Background data

- The bridge will support vehicle traffic only.

- The toll rate must be in whole peso increments. (All information given will be in terms of Argentine pesos, denoted by the $ symbol)

- Presently, 20,000 vehicles traveling between the two cities every day use a non-toll bridge 10 miles downriver.

- Your subcontractor conducted a field study and estimated the following values of time for the 20,000 vehicles currently using the free bridge:

Value ($/hour)	Number of Vehicles
10.00	5,000
5.00	10,000
2.50	5,000
TOTAL	20,000

- Vehicles using the free bridge travel an average of 40 miles per hour.

- Your subcontractor has estimated latent demand at three price points, in terms of vehicles per day (vpd):

    $3 toll rate: 500 vpd

    $2 toll rate: 2,000 vpd

    $1 toll rate: 5,000 vpd

- It will cost $30 million to build the bridge.

- Annual operating costs include $5 million in fixed maintenance, and 8 centavos per vehicle in variable maintenance.

- DevCo will own and operate the bridge in perpetuity.

- Assume no taxes.

- There is probably a difference in the cost of gas for a driver taking the toll bridge versus the non-toll bridge, since the distance traveled is different. For this analysis, assume that this difference is embedded in the value of time, so no additional calculations need to be made to account for gas. (Note to the interviewer: you might want to push interviewee to consider this issue by asking, "What other differences or issues do you see from the driver's perspective?")

- The company chooses to use a 20% discount rate to reflect both their cost of capital and the risk inherent in this type of project.

Suggested approach

Answering this question requires both a market sizing and a pricing analysis.

- First, the interviewee needs to determine how many vehicles could be expected to use the bridge.

- Secondly, the interviewee need to determine what price to charge for usage of the bridge, taking into account demand elasticity, required return on investment, and the competitive bidding process where the lowest bid will win.

Let's analyze the two sources of traffic volume on a new bridge: diversion of traffic from the existing alternate route, and latent demand.

1) **Diverted traffic** – The key to this case is to realize that vehicles will choose to use the new toll bridge if their cost savings from doing so is greater than the toll rate. A driver would compare the costs and benefits of using the closer but more expensive bridge. We can calculate that the new bridge saves drivers ½ hour (20 miles avoided at 40 miles per hour). Given the value of time information provided, we can generate a discrete demand curve:

~ $3 toll rate: 5,000 vehicles have cost savings of $5 per trip ($10/hour value of time * ½ hour time savings) and will use the new bridge

Visit the Vault Consulting Career Channel at **www.vault.com/consulting** — with insider firm profiles, message boards, the Vault Consulting Job Board and more.

VAULT CAREER LIBRARY **133**

~ $2 toll rate: An additional 10,000 vehicles have cost savings of $2.50 per trip ($5/hour value of time * ½ hour time savings) and will also use the new bridge at this price point.

~ $1 toll rate: An additional 5,000 vehicles have cost savings of $1.25 per trip ($2.50/hour value of time * ½ hour time savings) and will also use the new bridge at this price point.

2) **Latent demand** – It is more complicated to determine how many vehicles that do not presently cross the river would do so after the new bridge is built. The vehicle driver also perceives this decision from a cost-benefit standpoint, but the benefits are even less tangible than time savings, such as access to people, entertainment, or commercial opportunities not available on their own side of the river. An interview-based field study will support rough estimates of latent demand for use of a new bridge. The estimates given by the subcontractor represent a discrete demand curve and can be used directly in our calculations.

We can now calculate the revenue-maximizing toll rate by calculating the revenue for each toll rate, using what we know about both diverted demand and latent demand (the interviewer should ensure that the interviewee walks through these calculations extremely clearly):

- $3 toll rate: 5,000 vpd diverted demand + 500 vpd latent demand * $3 = $16,500/day

- $2 toll rate: (5,000 vpd + 10,000 vpd) diverted demand + 2,000 vpd latent demand * $2 = $34,000/day

- $1 toll rate: (5,000 vpd + 10,000 vpd + 5,000 vpd) diverted demand + 5,000 vpd latent demand * $1 = $25,000/day

Because the revenue is highest with the $2 toll rate, we can conclude that $2 is the revenue-maximizing toll rate.

Now, given our revenue estimate, let's calculate our return on investment.

1) Annual revenue = $34,000/day * 365 days = $12.4 million

2) Annual variable costs = 17,000 vpd * 365 days * $0.08/vehicle = $0.5m

3) Annual operating income = $12.4 m – $0.5m – $5m = $6.9m

4) Net present value = ($6.9m / 20%) – $30m = $4.5m

We see that this is a positive NPV project if we win the concession with a bid of a $2 toll rate.

Follow-up

Ask the interviewee to address issues involved in determining what toll rate to enter in a competitive bidding process:

- If the toll rate must be in whole-peso increments, it is likely that most participants will submit the same bid of $2. In order to have a positive NPV at either $1 or $3, one would have to assume substantially lower costs or higher volume. Therefore, we should consider what other factors can differentiate DevCo from the other bidders.

- An out-of-the-box suggestion is to recommend that DevCo negotiate a flexible toll rate schedule with the government to offload some risk. In this scenario, DevCo could raise the rate if demand is below expectations, and commit to lowering it if demand were higher than expected.

Finally, ask the interviewee to discuss risks involved in the project. These include:

- **Demand** – Traffic volume could be lower than expected. Both overall system volume could change, and the value of drivers' time could be incorrectly estimated.

- **Currency risk** – Is DevCo borrowing the required capital in US dollars? Will the peso toll rate be indexed to the US dollar? Are the drivers of maintenance costs denominated in the local currency, or does maintenance require imported goods and services?

- **Political risk** – The probability of expropriation or abrogation of concession contract terms should be evaluated when working in an emerging market.

- **Costs** – Cost overruns should always be a concern with a project of this scale.

How many consulting job boards have you visited lately?

(Thought so.)

Use the Internet's most targeted job search tools for consulting professionals.

Vault Consulting Job Board

The most comprehensive and convenient job board for consulting professionals. Target your search by area of consulting, function, and experience level, and find the job openings that you want. No surfing required.

VaultMatch Resume Database

Vault takes match-making to the next level: post your resume and customize your search by area of consulting, experience and more. We'll match job listings with your interests and criteria and e-mail them directly to your inbox.

PRESENTATION CASES

While the traditional case interview remains the tried-and-true method of screening potential consultants, many consulting firms are incorporating a hybrid interview into the mix: the presentation case. As a part of second or third round interview rounds, candidates may be ask to present and discuss a topic to a set of multiple interviewers.

The case interview presentation could take many different forms. You might be handed a pile of papers to read through and be instructed to put together a short PowerPoint deck for discussion in an hour. Some firms ask you to complete a set of presentation slides by hand, often supplying the conclusions and key insights based on the data provided. Other firms ask you to prepare a presentation ahead of time on the topic of your choice, and one or two even make you explain a topic to your interviewers on the fly.

As mentioned elsewhere in this guide, some consulting firms have been using presentations within the context of a group discussion and joint presentation for years. It is interesting to see that the trend is finally moving to the individual level.

Where is my case interview, and what have you done with it?

While the traditional case interview is generally a good indicator of success in actual problem-solving, it is also an imperfect assessment in many ways. Cracking a case on the spot isn't something you normally do on the job; in reality, you will rarely need to solve a client's problems in the space of twenty minutes. The necessary data would never be available right away, and you would have normally have days or weeks to create an appropriate framework and adjust it as necessary. Firms have realized that they might be missing out on great candidates who might not do well at in the classic case interview.

If you've taken a personality test like Myers-Briggs, you know by now that people process information differently. Some people are great at processing data using intuition; others need to have all of the facts and numbers before they can synthesize them. What if you weren't so great at analyzing a case on the fly and in front of a tense client, but with 10 minutes alone to reason you'd come up with a brilliant solution? Wouldn't that person make an outstanding consultant as well? Think about your peers who you feel would make highly successful consultants, yet aren't getting consulting jobs because they aren't stellar at case interviews.

From the firm's perspective, the presentation case interview can give the hiring firm data that the traditional case interview cannot provide. The firm gets a slightly better sense of how you might conduct yourself interacting with a client, which is generally just as high-pressure a situation (if not more) than your typical interview situation. It also sees you in a more typical job situation, where you are given data or research summaries and you need to draw some conclusions. Finally, the firm sees your presentation skills; no matter the level, nearly all consultants do at least some presenting on every project. This tells the firm quite a bit more about how you would actually do the job. This is so useful an interview format that you'd think most consulting firms would use it. Indeed, if it weren't so time-consuming (and therefore costly) for firms to round up the number of people necessary for this process, they probably would.

But this departure from the traditional case can also be a boon for the candidate. While there are a wide variety of traditional case interview questions out there, let us boldly argue that they test the same sorts of things – thinking on your feet, having studied and practiced frameworks, and having thought through the "right" types of problems. Here are just a few other dimensions or skills that could surface for you to better make your case:

- **Synthesizing research offline.** Suppose you were the sort of person described above, where you were decent at case interviews but exceptional at thinking about information and processing it after a few minutes alone? What if you were really good at spotting trends within a lot of data? The presentation case format could make you shine.

- **Presentation.** You also don't get the opportunity to present content during a traditional case interview that you get during a presentation case interview. Some people are really good at making presentations, and such speaking skills are crucial to client project work. An important aspect of this is presentation structuring.

- **Teaching ability.** Consultants are often the experts who have to teach content or explain complicated topics to clients. Again, during a traditional case interview you don't get the chance to show off your teaching skills, whereas during some versions of the presentation case interview you do.

- **Team skills.** Some firms are using the group interview format mixed into all of this; occasionally you will need to work with other interviewees to structure and present a recommendation to the mock review board. If you are particularly good at building team consensus and playing well in the sandbox, this will work in your favor.

The upshot is that you might have to do some or of all of these things during an interview. The fact is, you are going to have to do all of these things as a consultant. You might as well see what it's like to do some of them during the interview process. And you might get some extra points for it.

All in all, we think the presentation case interview is a good thing. It makes everyone in the process better informed, and that's better for everyone involved, especially you.

Common types

In sampling a solid fistful of recent interviewees for consulting firms, we have found a variety of presentation case interview types, including:

1) **Research case:** Study a set of client materials for half an hour, then present your findings to a mock client or project team, complete with Q&A.

2) **Complete the presentation:** You are given a partially-complete presentation that contains the findings and/or data, and you supply the insights.

3) **Teach me something:** Lecture or teach your interviewer about a topic of your choice (or theirs).

By far, the most common type of presentation case is the research case. We'll spend some extra time on this one and go through a full-blown example later.

General Tips and Tricks for All Presentation Cases

Presentation case interviews are therefore at the heart of it all an extension on the traditional case interview – different in structure and nature of what you analyze (reading versus listening), but at the end of the day, you still need to solve a business problem. To this end, here are some tips and tricks before we dive into some practice:

• **Make sure you are answering the right question.** There are presentation cases where you need to go into a room and think without the interaction of others. These are sometimes dangerous when you aren't sure what question to answer. If it's not clear, ask someone. If not, clearly state your assumed question at the beginning so your interviewers can put your answers into context.

• **Always try to establish ahead of time your presumed role and the presumed role of your audience.** If it is not clear based on the materials for some reason, state your assumption very matter-of-factly prior to commencing your presentation.

• **Watch the time!** Think about how much time you'll need to pull your talk together. Work backwards: subtract that amount of time from the total amount of time, and give yourself that much time to produce the slides or talk.

Presentation Case Type 1 – Research Case

Overview

As mentioned before, the most common type of presentation case is the kind where you receive a set of materials and are given a substantial amount of time to analyze the materials and create a short presentation to discuss with a mock project team or client board.

The materials given often include the following:

• Time-series data, such as revenues over time

• Visualization of data, such as pie charts, line graphs, stock price history, or bar charts

• Industry research

• Newspaper and journal articles

• Corporate press releases

• Web sites

You may be given anywhere from half an hour to an hour to synthesize this information.

In terms of actual presentation materials, some firms have you mock up a presentation on PowerPoint. Others will give you acetate slides and markers, or even flip charts and tape. It definitely varies. (Be ready to write neatly.)

How to approach it

Before you start any research case, realize that you are going to have to create a presentation by the time you leave the prep room. We recommend you first answer the question and then do the presentation part of it (which will be rather simple once you finish the analysis). Make you allocate plenty of time for production and stick to it!

That said, here is a general framework for tackling research presentation cases.

1) **Clarify the question.** What is the goal of the analysis? Are you to create a recommendation? Summarize the research and give next steps? Be clear on what your goal is. We would guess that you will usually be told what question you need to answer; sometimes you won't be, so you'll need to be prepared to formulate the question on your own.

2) **Skim the materials and isolate the two or three key sources of insight.** Now that you've clarified the question, you know what you're looking for. You might have time to read through everything, but you also might be pinched for time. In general, we recommend you first spend several minutes doing a fast review of all of the material. The key here is to not to understand exactly what everything says. You need to determine what information is relevant and what isn't – this is a key skill in business. When you're done, you should have a small pile of documents to provide the main support for your presentation and a list of key insights culled from the other documents.

3) **Build your framework.** This is the part you've already prepared for in working through the traditional case interview. It's the same here. What do you need to know to answer the question? If the question is how to improve profits, start with seeing how you would either increase revenue or decrease costs, which begs the possibilities of finding an optimal price/volume level, lowering fixed costs, or lowering variable costs. You have this one nailed already; nail it here.

4) **Crack the case.** Work through your framework and answer your questions. If you think about it, this is just like having the interviewer there to answer your questions, except you answer your questions by going to the key sources you identified earlier. Work until you either have as much information as you feel is necessary to answer the question or until you hit the time limit you previously set for yourself.

5) **Structure and create your presentation.** We will talk more about best practices for structuring presentations later. Our key types here use a "pyramid" method for structuring your talk. Start with an executive summary. Also, be sure you do at least a mental dry-run – envision yourself in front of the client and think through key phrases (jot those on a blank piece of paper to clutch during your talk – nothing wrong with notes).

Research Case Example: Pure Meats

In this comprehensive real-life example of a final round research case interview with a leading management consulting firm, you are given approximately 40 minutes to read through a set of materials, create a handwritten slide presentation, and present your findings to a panel of senior consultants pretending to be senior executives at the client company

The setup

You have been told in advance over the phone by HR that one of the final round interviews will involve presenting. The HR person explains that you will play the role of the consultant, and a number of senior firm executives will play the role of the board of directors receiving your presentation.

On your interview day, you have a fit interview with one of the partners. You are then are ushered into a conference room with the following materials:

- Stack of paper documents (we'll get to these in a second)
- Stack of documents on slide materials that can be used on an overhead projector
- Blank acetate pages that can be used on an overhead projector
- Dry erase markers

You are told to imagine that you are a consultant who has just taken a first look at the attached documents for a client named Pure Meats, who makes prepackaged raw meat for retail distribution. Pure, it turns out, is concerned about a new product from a competitor, Gordon, who has been making steady inroads into Pure's market share. Today the Board of Directors is onsite for the day, and they want to hear your initial thoughts on the issues. In advance of your conversation with the board, you are to take 40 minutes to read through the given materials and create a handwritten slide presentation using the materials provided. Afterwards, you will present your findings to the Board of Directors, and undergo a Q&A session.

Getting ready

First, let's get organized and inventory our documents. (See Figures 1-10.)

- Introductory page describing the case interview situation.

- Newspaper article detailing how Gordon Meats entered the retail beef market last year and has had amazing success with their pre-cooked beef.

- Tables showing market share of the client company (Pure Meats) and its competitors over time for different products: beef, chicken, and pork.

- Internal memo from a Pure Meats processing plant manager to HQ stating that he has some 50% excess capacity available, and pointing out that with another plant coming online in a few months, there will be a lot of idle capacity.

- Pie chart showing Pure's percentage of sales from its different products.

- Summary of a customer segmentation analysis done by another consulting firm.

- Pure Meats stock price history showing almost perfect correlation with the S&P. (Note no precipitous drop after Gordon entered the market and started stealing share).

- Graph of U.S. retail meat consumption per capita over time – beef, chicken, fish.

- Graph of total U.S. retail meat consumption over time – beef, chicken, and fish.

- Newspaper article explaining how the U.S. public has become more health-conscious in recent years, and is worried about saturated fat in beef.

- Perceptual map of beef competitors based on customer focus groups.

This is also the right time to establish timing. Set aside at least 10 minutes at the end to put together your talk (five minutes to put together a few bullet point slides and five minutes to think through your presentation). Stick to it. If you get more time than that, great; if not, you will need all 10 of those minutes.

Visit the Vault Consulting Career Channel at **www.vault.com/consulting** — with
insider firm profiles, message boards, the Vault Consulting Job Board and more.

VAULT CAREER LIBRARY   **145**

Approach

Let's work through our five-step framework

1. Clarify the question

2. Skim the materials and isolate the key sources of insight

3. Build your framework

4. Crack the case

5. Structure and create your presentation

Step 1: Clarify the question

What does it mean to "assess the viability" of a competitor that is already in the market? That is, under what conditions would Gordon be a true long-term threat to Pure? You would need to see two conditions:

- **Current situation:** Gordon had started to erode Pure's revenue in its key segments or products

- **Future situation:** Given market dynamics, Gordon will continue to be better positioned than Pure and this trend will continue

You will need to make an assumption as to what your value measure is. Your guess is that the client isn't worried about profits as much as a drop in revenue. What about market share? Not sure. (Quiz question: is declining market share ever okay? We'll address this later.)

One other thing to recognize here: you are probably going to be able to figure out if Pure should be worried about Gordon; however, you are probably not going to reach a recommendation regarding what you should do about it. You should offer either a hypothesis or a set of alternatives, plus next steps on how to move forward. Therefore, you are going to:

1. Answer the question of whether Gordon poses a real threat.

2. Suggest (and discuss) possible recommendations without evaluating them.

You can see now that it's very important to get the question right! Now you can focus on what matters.

Step 2: Skim the materials and isolate the key sources of insight

Now that you know what you're looking for, you can dive deeper into the materials. Not including the cover sheet, there are ten sheets of paper in front of you. This seems pretty overwhelming. Let's address the figures one by one and see if we can focus our analysis a bit.

Figure 1: The article excerpt notes that Gordon entered the market in 2002 with a pre-cooked beef product and seems to be doing well. You should immediately think to yourself, "So what? Who would buy such a product?" Your intuition should tell you that this is probably a great product for people in a rush with a busy lifestyle, but wouldn't appeal to chefs and traditional cooks. Jot this thought down on your page of notes.

Figure 1: Excerpt from article in the Door Street Journal

Milwaukee, WI (AP) – When Gordon Meat Company entered the retail beef market in 2002 with its novel pre-cooked beef product, few expected the company to make inroads into an industry heavily dominated by long-time leader Pure Meats. After a little over one year, Gordon already has a market share of 27% of the US beef market—and Pure's customers have been the major source of Gordon's.

"Gordon seems to have tapped into a widespread phenomenon of people wanting to spend less time cooking, likely because they are busy," said Greg Rooke, an equity analyst at Jones and Company, an investment bank. "You have to wonder how the other market players, especially Pure, will react."

Figure 2: This is a comparison of market shares. You will probably want to take a look at this one in more depth.

Figure 2: Meat Industry Market Shares 2001-2003

Company	Pure Meats	Meat Street	Cattle Tales	Gordon	All Others
2001 Market Share in Beef	72%	5%	4%	--	19%
2001 Market Share in Chicken	20%	15%	12%	--	53%
2001 Market Share in Pork	18%	14%	13%	--	55%
2002 Market Share in Beef	72%	5%	4%	2%	17%
2002 Market Share in Chicken	20%	15%	12%	0%	53%
2002 Market Share in Pork	18%	14%	13%	0%	55%
2003 Market Share in Beef	52%	4%	3%	27%	13%
2003 Market Share in Chicken	19%	15%	12%	0%	54%
2003 Market Share in Pork	19%	14%	13%	0%	54%

Figure 3: A memo, the salient point of which is that Pure Meats has enough manufacturing capacity to introduce a new product or increase production on a current product. Not much more to this figure than that point. Jot it down and move on.

Figure 3: Internal Memo from Pure Meats

TO: Pure Meats Headquarters

FROM: Kevin Klein, Pure Meat Processing Plant Manager

SUBJECT: Results of capacity study

We have completed our analysis of the availability of capacity at the Pure Meats processing plant. Our findings are attached to this cover sheet.

In summary, we have determined that we currently have 50% excess capacity available. In addition, with another plant coming online in a few months, we estimate that we will have nearly 70% idle capacity .

(Attachments have been deleted)

Figure 4: You can see that Pure Meats sells packaged, uncooked beef, chicken, and pork, with beef being its primary product at nearly 80% of its revenues. The main point is that Pure Meats' main product is beef, so it will be concerned about a new competitor. Jot the point down.

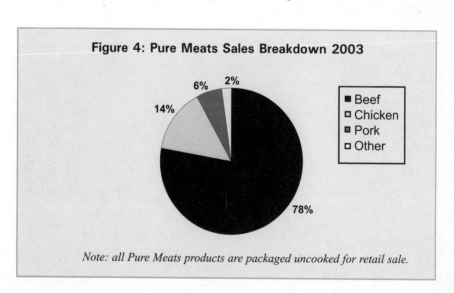

Figure 4: Pure Meats Sales Breakdown 2003

- Beef
- Chicken
- Pork
- Other

6% 2% 14% 78%

Note: all Pure Meats products are packaged uncooked for retail sale.

Figure 5: This one seems to have a lot of information in it about customer segmentation. Since we're dealing with revenues, we probably need to think hard about to whom we're selling. Set this aside to look at later in depth.

Figure 5: Segmentation of beef consumers

Segment	Sales Channels		Size of segment as % of Revenue 2003	Projected annual growth of segment, 2004-2009	Company with greatest concentration of sales in segment*
	Large grocery stores	High-priced specialty shops			
Traditional grandmothers	✔		50%	-5%	Pure
Busy moms	✔	✔	15%	20%	Gordon
Gourmets		✔	5%	5%	Gordon
Price-conscious	✔		30%	5%	Mixed

Figure 6: There seem to be two main points to this chart. For the most part, the Pure Meats stock tracks the S&P, and Pure Meats' stock price wasn't impacted too much by the entrance of Gordon. There's not much more to it than that.

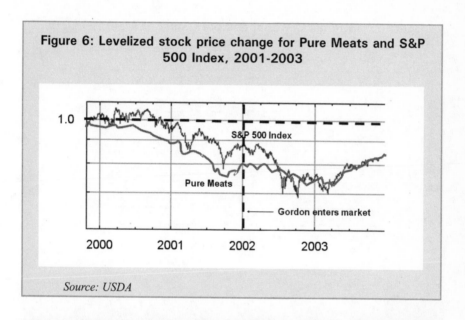

Figure 6: Levelized stock price change for Pure Meats and S&P 500 Index, 2001-2003

Source: USDA

Figure 7: This seems helpful. It shows that beef consumption per person is actually on the decline, while chicken consumption per person is skyrocketing. Fish is increasing slightly. Keep this.

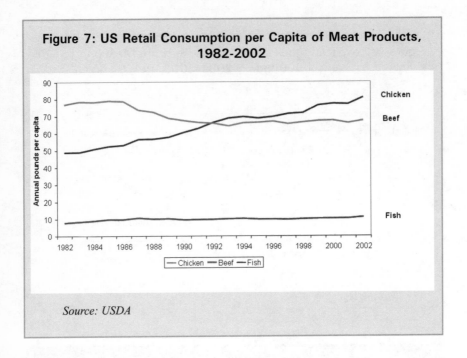

Figure 7: US Retail Consumption per Capita of Meat Products, 1982-2002

Source: USDA

Figure 8: Total U.S. consumption is actually more useful than consumption per head, because it tells you the size of the total market in pounds, as segmented by meat type. (It's essentially the previous chart scaled appropriately for population growth.) In the interest of time, let's keep Figure 8 and put Figure 7 back in the pile. Also, you should hear a little warning bell go off in your head that you can link this figure to Figure 2, which contained the market shares.

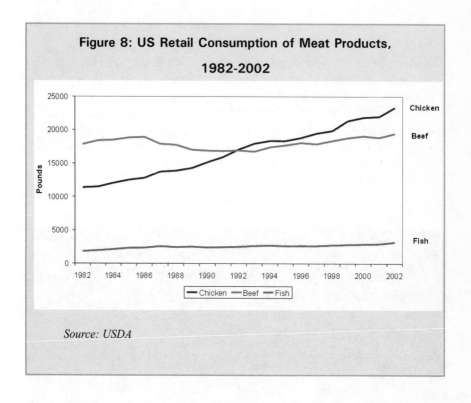

Figure 8: US Retail Consumption of Meat Products, 1982-2002

Source: USDA

Visit the Vault Consulting Career Channel at **www.vault.com/consulting** — with insider firm profiles, message boards, the Vault Consulting Job Board and more.

V/\ULT CAREER LIBRARY   **153**

Figure 9: This seems like a rationale for the previous chart – people are becoming more health conscious, and because chicken contains lower cholesterol than beef, chicken is becoming very popular (as is fish). Jot down the point and move on.

Figure 9: Article from Door Street Journal

Omaha, NE (AP) – Studies show that the US public has become more health conscious in recent years. In particular, the US public is more worried about saturated fat in beef.

"Heart disease rates are on the rise," says Dr. Hal E. Walker, a cardiology professor at Harbored Medical School. "When Lipitor, a cholesterol-lowering drug, is the top-selling drug in the country, you know that the public is highly aware of these issues."

Indeed, beef consumption has been on the decline in recent years, supplanted largely by chicken — which has considerably less saturated fat—and somewhat by fish.

Figure 10: Have you ever seen a perceptual map before? If you're an MBA, you no doubt saw it in your marketing class. If you're at the undergrad level, you may or may not have seen it in your psychology class. In a nutshell: a perceptual map displays and differentiates customers' views of products along key, distinct dimensions. It's that simple, and that useful. You could have inferred this but this lays it out: in the beef market, Pure Meats is huge on quality, while Gordon is all about convenience. Save this.

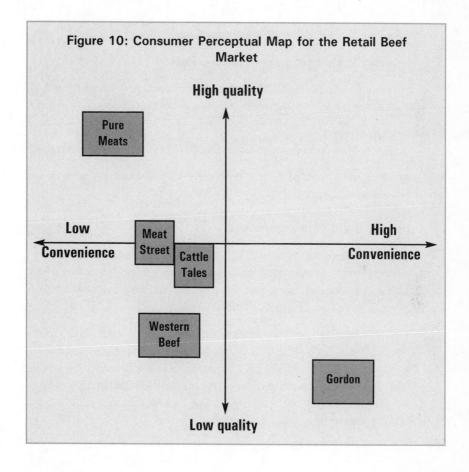

Figure 10: Consumer Perceptual Map for the Retail Beef Market

You've been through all of the information, and here's what you have:

• Four figures: 2, 5, 8, and 10. One more than you had hoped, but it will have to do.

• A sheet of notes with the following points:

  • Gordon's product is a great product for people in a rush with a busy lifestyle, but doesn't appeal to the purist chefs and traditional family cooks. (Figure 1)

  • Pure Meats could easily double production. (Figure 3)

  • Pure Meats' biggest market is beef. (Figure 4)

  • People are becoming more health conscious, and because chicken contains lower cholesterol than beef, chicken is becoming very popular (as is fish).

  • Pure Meats is huge on quality, while Gordon is all about convenience.

Much better! Now, pull out a fresh piece of paper and get to work on processing this stuff.

Step 3: Build your framework

The point of this step is to help you organize your thinking. You probably could have done this prior to Step 2, but after going through Step 2, you're a little more educated now about what matters and you can now create a targeted way of working through the information.

Earlier in this book, we learned about different kinds of frameworks – cost-benefit, Porters, etc. What kind of structure makes sense given the question we are trying to answer? This is a good time to craft a strategy for yourself. You could choose to either go in depth on one thing or summarize everything superficially. Or you might choose to come up with a creative hook, e.g. go into the chicken business as a hedge.

Here is one possible framework:

• External situation

  – Market dynamics: how is the market responding to Gordon?

  – Competition: Does Gordon seem like a threat to our revenue or market position based on current data?

• Company response / potential recommendations

    – Define and prioritize alternatives

    – Assess company capabilities and resources

• Next step (time permitting)

    – Evaluate alternatives

    – Measure against capabilities and resources

(Bonus question: try this case again using a different framework.)

Step 4: Crack the case

You have your framework, you have all of the information. Now let's tackle the question head on.

• External situation

    – In terms of market dynamics, there are at least three points of note. You may see others.

      1. It looks like the market is responding very well to Gordon. Look at market share in Figure 2. Pure's market share in 2002 was the same as in 2001, but then in 2003 Pure's market share in beef dropped 20 points to 52%. Scan the other rows and you'll see that Gordon has an additional 20 points of market share in beef. A trap would be to immediately assume that Gordon took over Pure's market share, but what if the market grew enough such that Pure's market share went from 72% to 52% but Pure's revenue stayed the same? (Quick question: by how much would the market have had to grow for this to be the case?) It turns out that this is not the case; as per Figure 8, the beef market is actually not growing very much. It's safe to assume that Gordon indeed has stolen Pure's market share.

      2. According to Figure 5, Gordon's key segment for its precooked beef product is the small but fast-growing "busy mom" segment. This assumes that it takes less time to prepare a meal using precooked beef versus raw beef; this seems reasonable.

      3. Finally, chicken consumption is well ahead of beef consumption and is continuing to rise while beef consumption remains flat. We can see this very clearly in Figure 8. Figure 9 gives some rationale for the switch to chicken (health).

    – What can we say about Gordon as competition?

1. Gordon does appear to be a long-term threat to Pure Meat's market position in beef.

2. Gordon has taken over the "busy mom" segment, which is definitely growing fast. (Bonus question: based on these growth rates, when does the "busy mom" segment exceed the "traditional grandmother" segment?)

3. Gordon's success is especially troubling for Pure Meats because Pure is so heavily concentrated in beef.

4. Therefore, Gordon does appear to be a long-term threat to Pure Meat's market position in beef. Pure Meat needs to react appropriately.

• What should the Pure Meat company response be?

– We can brainstorm alternatives. There are some fairly standard alternatives that we can consider. Can we rule any of these out? Let's make a laundry list.

1. Do nothing – this seems like a bad option. We should rule this out.

2. Offer a competing product – we could definitely consider going head-to-head with Gordon using a copy of its product. We could consider this.

3. Attempt to buy Gordon – a possibility if we have the capital. It's a question to raise.

4. Attempt to partner with Gordon – a possibility because we don't offer competing products. On the other hand, is this so useful if our beef product doesn't fit the shift in customer preferences? Maybe there aren't any synergies to be had.

5. Enter the chicken market to counter the decline in the demand for beef – This is a good suggestion. We don't know what's involved, and we don't know how such an entry would be perceived. Entry could be build or buy – maybe a new brand?

6. Other out-of-the-box ideas – Gordon's marketing chief is doing a great job, so maybe we should hire her. Another idea: could we offer our company up for sale to Gordon?

– Following our framework, let's think through company capabilities and resources. We actually don't have much information on this yet, so let's make a list of items we want to ask about

1. **Capacity** – Do we have available capacity if we want to branch off into a new product?

2. **Cash situation** – if we wanted to buy Gordon, could we do it? How would we finance it?

3. **Management and shareholders** – would they be open to partnership, purchase, etc.?

4. **Other resources** – do we have the right staff?

- Next steps – you've probably run out of time by now and should get cracking on creating the presentation, but take a minute and think through what needs to happen next:

  – Evaluate alternatives

  – Assess company capabilities and resources

  – Create a marketing plan that incorporates distribution, channels, and target marketing

  – Can you think of other next steps? Jot these down quickly and move on

Step 5: Structure and create the presentation

With ten or so minutes left, it's time to build the short presentation. It's not uncommon for companies to make you do the presentation using transparencies versus Powerpoint; it's probably to level the playing field, as some people are fast at putting together Powerpoint and others are not. Everyone can scribble chicken scratch onto a slide. It doesn't have to be clean; your interviewers are judging structure and clarity of thought.

First structure your thoughts, then practice building your presentation on blank sheets of printer paper. The presentation might be structured as follows:

- Executive summary

- Situation (1-2 slides)

- Alternatives

- Next steps

We've created a sample version of the presentation. Obviously, your presentation will look different. We suggest that you do follow some best practices culled from the consulting world:

- Start with your executive summary, so your audience knows where you are headed and can take in subsequent information appropriately.

- The slide titles should all be complete sentences. When read in sequence, they should tell you the complete story.

- Bullet points on each slide should support the slide title. Try not to have more than three bullets per page.

- Sometimes it helps to have subject tags on each slide, e.g. situation or alternatives. This helps your audience know where you are in the presentation.

- Look for places where a visual could tell the story better. Note our first situation slide. The two key market dimensions were healthiness and convenience and so a 2x2 shows the market dynamics.

- A box at the bottom of a slide could be effective for conveying a key question to the audience or the main takeaway of the slides. (See the "alternatives" slide.)

- Write big enough that an audience member can read the slide from afar.

Last thought: if you are pressed for time, you can get by with just two slides: summary of situation, and alternatives. You can speak about the rest of the information as it comes up.

Notes on delivering the presentation

It's game time! The HR representative is walking you to the mock Board of Directors meeting. Here are some final tips and guidelines for the conversation:

- **Framing is key**. Set the expectation for what you're going to talk about. For example: "Thank you to the Board for making time for our discussion today. I've received the market research recently and have just looked it over. I'd like to communicate a summary of what I've learned thus far and think through where we would go from here." The Board should not expect you to come up with a recommendation after this framing statement.

- **Be ready for Q&A.** Expect that your presentation will be more like a discussion than a lecture. The Board may want to drill down on some of your points, or ask for clarification. Have your notes and key exhibits available for reference.

• **Remember the basics.** Just like in your usual case interview, monitor yourself for things like eye contact, smiles, posture, overall demeanor, and a slow, steady pacing of your voice.

• **Relax!** There is absolutely no reason to be scared. Treat the presentation like an important conversation that you've done some solid prep for. You've earned this opportunity to show your stuff and you're ready for it.

Here's what your final presentation might look like:

Executive Summary

We should be concerned about Gordon as a viable competitor to Pure Meats and should craft a response

• Gordon's pre-cooked beef meets a growing market need for a more convenient meat product

• Gordon's product has made significant inroads into Pure's market share in beef

    - Beef has traditionally been Pure's largest market

• We have brainstormed a number of alternatives that we suggest evaluating versus the company capabilities as a next step

Visit the Vault Consulting Career Channel at **www.vault.com/consulting** — with insider firm profiles, message boards, the Vault Consulting Job Board and more.

VAULT CAREER LIBRARY   **161**

Situation

Market research suggests that in the retail meat market, customer preferences are shifting based on demand for healthier, more convenient products.

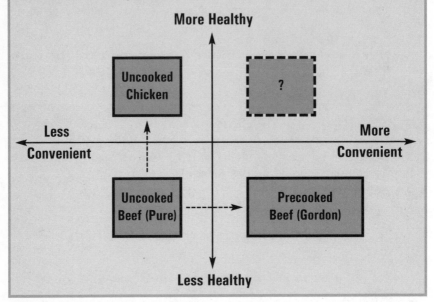

Situation

Gordon seems to have capitalized on this trend in the beef market, but not in the fast-growing chicken market.

- From 2002 to 2003, Pure Meats' market share in beef dropped from 72% to 52%

- Gordon's market share increased from 2% to 27% in the same period

    - Because the overall size of the beef market has remained very flat over time, it seems that Gordon has taken over Pure's market share in beef

- The chicken market remains open

    - Likely because it is a healthy alternative to beef, chicken consumption continues to increase substantially

    - Gordon has not come out with a similar chicken product

Alternatives

There are a number of possible responses.

- High priority alternatives

    - Copy Gordon with a pre-cooked beef product

    - Retain positioning with raw meat but enter the chicken market

- Other alternatives

    - Do nothing

    - Buy Gordon

    - Partner with Gordon

Are there other alternatives the Board feels we should consider?

Next Steps

We propose a series of next steps.

- Clarify and evaluate alternatives

- Assess company capabilities versus these alternatives

- Craft implementation plan

Presentation Case Type 2 – Complete the Presentation

An increasingly common variation on the presentation case requires you to complete a set of slides for a client presentation, then discuss the results and key insights with a mock client or project team.

Unlike the research case, this type of case generally tests how well you can distill information into conclusions. It also may involve analysis questions that are more involved and require further depth than most questions on the research case.

For these cases, it is vitally important that you not only complete the slides, but that you are able to demonstrate a strong grasp of the overall client situation. During the discussion following your work session, you will likely need to:

- Summarize the client situation

- State the key insights and show what data or calculations support those insights

- Raise further implications for the client beyond the analysis

- Discuss potential recommendations

Complete the Presentation Example: Wells Incorporated

On the next few pages, we have provided an example of a presentation case where you are required to complete the slides and derive key insights. We suggest you photocopy the following seven pages, sit in a quiet room, and work through the case. When you are finished, read through the suggested solutions carefully to see how you did. Be sure to think through the "Additional Insights for Discussion" as well.

For even better practice, we suggest having a friend play the role of the client. Your friend should read through the full set of case materials, including the solutions and page of additional insights. (Don't look at the solutions or insights ahead of time.) After you have finished your work, walk through your completed presentation for your friend, allowing him or her to ask questions along the way. Have your friend raise each of the issues listed on the "Additional Insights for Discussion" page. Good luck!

Case Interview: Wells Incorporated

Your client is an oil company called Wells Incorporated. Wells owns six medium-sized oil tankers that are used to transport thousands of barrels of oil for other companies. Wells Inc. wants to invest in new equipment and is seeking to sell off its oil tankers in order to raise money.

Based on current demand for oil transportation, the oil tankers collectively earn steady revenues of $450,000 per year. However, profitability of these tankers is very low. Buyers perceive low profitability to be a function of excess capacity; therefore, there have been no takers to buy the ships.

The client has engaged your team to clarify the economic story behind the oil tanker industry as a means of crafting an alternative divestiture strategy. Your team has consolidated a fair amount of economic analysis, and you need to finish pulling the information together for a client discussion within the hour.

Part A: A summary of the industry research appears on the next four slides, which need to be completed. Please review the background information contained in the first slide, then follow the instructions on the following three slides to complete the analysis.

Part B: After much brainstorming, the partner on your project has suggested an alternative means of raising capital. His hypothesis is that if you retire five of the ships, there will be less or no excess capacity in the industry, prices would rise, and then the remaining ship will be profitable. Please complete the test of this hypothesis on slides four and five.

You will be discussing this presentation in half an hour with your client team. Please be prepared for a discussion with your team around the presentation content and other issues important to the business problem. You will be meeting with them in approximately 30 minutes. Good luck!

Part A: Background information on the oil transport industry

- Oil shipping is a *commodity* industry

    - There is strong competition and little differentiation among ships

    - Pricing is very close to the cost of supply for the marginal supplier

    - Each trip earns the same revenue per barrel, which is set by determining the *market clearing price* that matches supply and demand

- All ships in the industry are subject to the same features and regulations

    - Each ship is independently owned and is capable of exactly one trip per year

    - Ships can be small, medium, or large (see next page)

    - All ships are currently registered with the Oil Transport Commission, which tracks official oil shipping capacity and demand. Registered ships have the option but not the obligation to embark on trips. Ships can be retired or registered at any time for a nominal fee.

    - A ship's owner will not engage in oil transport unless a trip is at least break-even.

    - Variable costs are the only costs per trip

    - Effectively, a ship lasts forever – there is no depreciation on these ships, and a used ship costs exactly the same as a new ship

    - A ship's discount rate over time is 5%

Part A: Supply Information – Ship Data

Size of Ship	Number of Ships	Capacity per Ship (Thousands of Barrels)	Cost per Trip	Effective Cost per Barrel
Small	30	50	$50,000	
Medium	15	100	$75,000	
Large	10	200	$0	

Part A: Supply, Demand, and Market Clearing Price

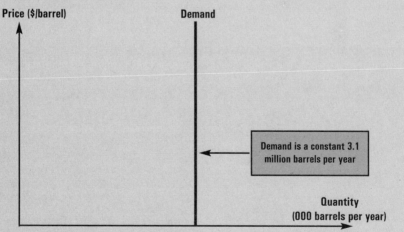

Price ($/barrel)

Demand

Demand is a constant 3.1 million barrels per year

Quantity (000 barrels per year)

Note to candidate: using the information on the previous slide, please construct the supply curve for this industry. When you are done, you should be able to determine the **market-clearing equilibrium price per barrel**.

Part A: Wells Incorporated Profit Calculation

Size of Ship	Number of Ships	Capacity per Ship (000 Barrels)	Market Clearing Price ($/Barrel)	Total Revenue per Year ($)	Total Cost per Year ($)	Profit/Loss per Year ($)
Medium	6	100				

Key Takeaway:

Note to candidate: using the information contained on the previous two slides, please calculate the blank fields leading to the total annual profit for Wells Inc. In the box above, please write a one-sentence summary explaining what is causing this level of profitability.

Suggested Solutions – Wells Incorporated

Part A: Supply Information – Ship Data

Size of Ship	Number of Ships	Capacity per Ship (Thousands of Barrels)	Cost per Trip	Effective Cost per Barrel
Small	30	50	$50,000	$1.00
Medium	15	100	$75,000	$0.75
Large	10	200	$100,000	$0.50

Part A: Supply, Demand, and Market Clearing Price

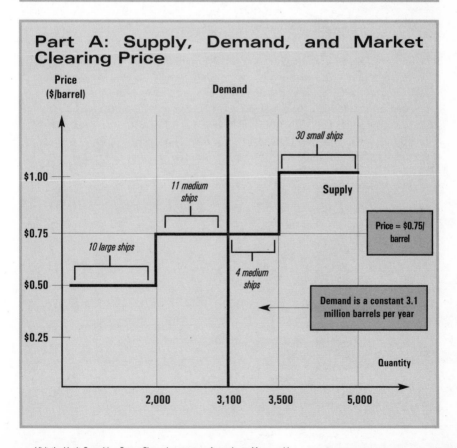

Visit the Vault Consulting Career Channel at **www.vault.com/consulting** — with
insider firm profiles, message boards, the Vault Consulting Job Board and more.

VAULT CAREER LIBRARY   **169**

Part A: Summary of Profitability

Size of Ship	Number of Ships	Capacity per Ship (000 Barrels)	Market Clearing Price ($/Barrel)	Total Revenue per Year ($)	Total Cost per Year ($)	Expected Profit/Loss per Year ($)
Medium	6	100	$0.75	$450,000*	$450,000*	$0

Illustrative key takeaway (there are several possible answers)

> Excess capacity in the industry is driving prices down, making small ships unprofitable and medium ships break-even.

*Another acceptable answer would calculate both of these values as $330,000 instead of $450,000. The case is deliberately unclear as to whether Wells' 6 ships are among the 11 medium ships that are required to fill demand. A reasonable assumption would be that any medium ship has a 11/15 chance of running a trip, so the expected revenue for Wells is 6 x 100,000 x $0.75 x (11/15) = $330,000, while the expected cost is 6 x $75,000 x (11/15) = $330,000, so the expected profit is $330,000 – $330,000 = $0. The point of Part A is to conclude that the ships net no profit, so either answer is fine.

Part A: Supply, Demand, and Market Clearing Price

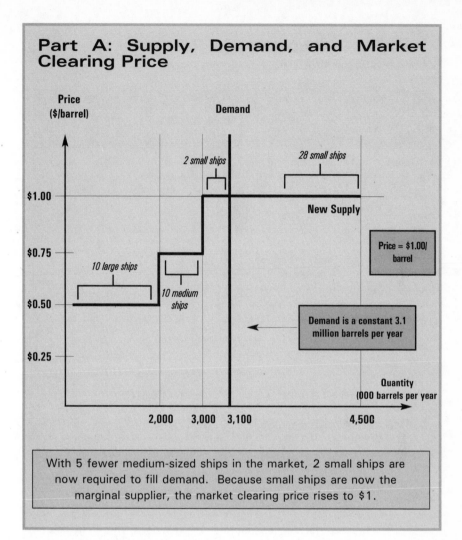

With 5 fewer medium-sized ships in the market, 2 small ships are now required to fill demand. Because small ships are now the marginal supplier, the market clearing price rises to $1.

Visit the Vault Consulting Career Channel at **www.vault.com/consulting** — with
insider firm profiles, message boards, the Vault Consulting Job Board and more.

VAULT CAREER LIBRARY   **171**

Part B: Summary of Profitability with Retired Capacity

Size of Ship	Number of Ships	Capacity per Ship (000 Barrels)	Market Clearing Price ($/Barrel)	Total Revenue per Year ($)	Total Cost per Year ($)	Expected Profit/Loss per Year ($)
Medium	1	100	$1.00	$100,000	$75,000	$25,000

Illustrative key takeaway (there are several possible answers)

Retiring the excess capacity allows Wells Inc. to sell oil transport at a higher price per barrel and improve profits to $25,000 per year.

Additional Insights for Discussion

- Retiring the ships without getting rid of them retains the real option to revive them, should prices rise even further. This gives the owner the potential to earn even more profits in the industry

    – Where would the client store the inactive ships?

- The client has choices—which is better for the client?

    – Retire the five ships, but keep the remaining ship to generate cashflow (not useful if the client needs lots of upfront cash)

    – Attempt to divest the six ships as a package using the retirement/real option analysis as a sales pitch

- What would be a fair price at which to sell the package of ships?

    – The annual profit from the single active ship is $25,000 per year

    – Use the discount rate of 5% to calculate the value of this perpetuity: value = $25,000/0.05 = $500,000

Presentation Case Type 3 – Teach Me Something

A final twist on the presentation case interview involves explaining to your interviewer how something works. Here are some activities your interviewer might ask you to do:

- Teach your interviewer a skill

- Prepare a presentation in advance and be ready to answer questions

- Complete a presentation that contains the findings and/or data – you supply the insights

- Explain a complex topic to your interviewer

These presentation cases are more about the process than the content. In other words, it's less about what you teach than how you teach it. Some best practices for getting the process right are as follows:

- **Introduce the topic and objective.** Be sure not to just plunge into your discussion without framing of the conversation – what are we going to talk about today?

- **Explain why the topic is worth learning about.** Why would this be useful to know? Why should you listen to me and engage in a dialogue? This is a very important component of the setup. As part of the motivation, if you're teaching a useful skill, demonstrate the skill or show an example of the final product up front.

- **Communicate the structure of your talk.** Tell the audience what you're going to talk about, then talk about it. A roadmap for your audience helps them follow along.

- **Give the right level of detail.** If you are explaining a complex topic, keep it at a high level. If you are explaining a relatively simple topic, discuss the nuances of it to make it more interesting.

- **Dialogue with your audience.** Check in to make sure that your audience is getting it and is interested. Ask questions – have you seen/done this before? Can you think of a way this might be useful? Does that make sense to you? Try to build a relationship with your audience.

Below are some examples of topics you could teach or explain. We suggest you take the time now to think through one or two topics you could teach with preparation and one or two topics you could be ready to teach on the spot.

Business topics

- Use of Black Scholes equation for pricing a European option
- How to assess whether a stock is overvalued
- Explain how carbon dioxide results in global warming
- Use of Porter's Five Forces to analyze an industry
- Should I rent or buy a house?
- How does the clinical trial work for drug development?

How stuff works

- How electricity is produced
- How an airplane stays in the air
- How digital radio works
- How carbon dioxide production results in global warming
- The physics of Olympic curling

History and social issues

- Explain the reasons why the Soviet Union collapsed
- Explain how WWI started
- Why is college tuition increasing?
- Explain deconstructionism or another complex critical theory

Music and art

- Overview of the different artistic genres or periods
- Music theory basics

Creative ideas

- Learn to draw animals
- How to play smart billiards
- What is the efficient travel path from one place to another?
- Make a paper animal using origami
- Flip a pen around your fingers
- Do a yoga pose

- Cook something complex (use diagrams and/or explain the chemistry behind it)

Difficult Situation Cases

A recent interviewee at a leading strategy consulting firm reported that of her four second round on-site interviews, two were with partners who did not give her a business case. Instead, they talked more about situations that the interviewee had been in where she had to confront difficult people or resolve a challenging organizational situation.

As consulting firms strive to create less cutthroat working cultures, they are placing increased emphasis on fit and interpersonal skills. As a result, interviewers are asking questions where the case deals not with a business situation like falling revenues, but a challenging interpersonal situation. Examples of such situations are:

- Confronting a co-worker whom seems to be not getting the work done on your project

- Dealing with unethical behavior by a client

- Coping with family emergencies while on the job

These are important situations and important questions. Most consulting candidates shoot from the hip on such questions and don't prepare for them, focusing on the usual cases instead. They run the risk of communicating unstructured, scattered answers. Why create this impression for your interviewer? We recommend you prepare for them in the way you would prepare for case interviews: think about how you would approach these problems in general, then practice.

How would you approach these situations in real life? Step outside of some actual incidents that happened to you and pretend to be coaching yourself on the steps you needed to take to get it resolved. How would you describe these steps as applicable to any situation? After a few minutes, you'll probably come up with something similar to the following:

- Assess the *situation*

- Determine what other *information* you'll need to draw a conclusion

- Decide on the best course of *action* towards resolving the issue

- Immediately move forward with the appropriate *communication*

• If necessary, proceed with *escalation* to a higher or external authority

You might wonder if it is really necessary to create a "framework" for such questions. By that, you probably mean we shouldn't need frameworks to solve personal situations. Unfortunately, those are probably the ones where we need frameworks the most. In many ways these are harder problems to solve. And given how hard they are to solve, their solutions are probably even harder to communicate than those regarding profit and loss.

A final thought before we dive in: the case scenarios all reflect real situations that might occur during your first couple of years on the job. Our hope is that while you practice answering these questions, you also wind up preparing for how you will handle these situations when they come up in real life. Tackle these problems as you would the client issue: take a step back, assess the situation, come up with an approach, and give it your best shot.

Difficult Situation Case #1: Work Styles

You're an associate at Marathon Associates, and you are working with another associate on a project. You have become frustrated because you are working night and day on a very demanding project, while your colleague seems to be coming in late every day, leaving early, and spending a lot of time on the phone. After one day on client site, the client commented to you on the differences in work styles he has observed. You don't feel your colleague is pulling her weight on the project team. What should you do?

You:	First of all, I am very happy to be working on such a challenging project – I certainly don't mind the long hours! However, I am concerned that the client actually mentioned this issue to me. I'd like to ask a few clarifying questions. How unhappy was the client about my fellow associate's work style?
Interviewer:	Actually, the client merely commented on the differences in work styles, but didn't make any overt criticism of either of you.
You:	I see. I'm glad to hear that. So, if we have an issue, it hasn't yet risen to the level of making a bad impression on our client. In that case, since you have told me I am already frustrated with the situation, I would want to speak with my colleague as soon as possible, before I

build up any more frustration. Maybe I can ask her to grab a sandwich with me for lunch tomorrow, and bring up my concerns.

Interviewer:	So, you are going to confront your associate directly? Would you talk to your project manager first?
You:	That's a consideration, but it sounds like it might not be enough a crisis yet to involve my project manager. Plus, I think it's always best to simply address people directly as a first step. Let me ask you: do I have a good working relationship with my colleague?
Interviewer:	Let's say it's neutral – this is the first project you've worked on together.
You:	OK, then I think it's best that we simply meet for lunch, and I'll bring up the issue delicately. After all, it's possible that I've somehow misinterpreted my colleague's comings and goings. A constructive, non-judgmental way to start would be to say that I'm concerned about our team being able meeting the project deadlines, given how many hours we are working.
Interviewer:	Let's say I'm your colleague. I'm surprised when you say that. I don't think we'll have any problem meeting the deadlines.
You:	I'm certainly glad to hear that vote of confidence. I'm working 16-hour days, and there aren't many more hours in the day I can dedicate to work. Do you feel that you are working long hours as well?
Interviewer:	Yes, but that's just the way it goes in consulting.
You:	Hmm. I know we don't overlap too many hours at the project site. Are you working a lot of hours from home perhaps?
Interviewer:	Actually, yes, I am. Why do you ask?
You:	I've been feeling like I'm putting in a lot of work on this project, and I guess I just haven't been clear on what everyone else's role has been. It sounds like you and I may have different work styles: I tend to stay at the project site until I finish the day's work, and you tend to

work from home a lot, I guess. Can I ask if you've worked with this client before, and if you know what their preference is for our on-site work hours?

Interviewer: OK, good. I can tell you that your colleague has worked with this client for the past year. How would you resolve the situation?

You: I would want to talk through a few more issues with the colleague: (1) understand what the client's expectations are based on our prior project work style, (2) discuss the project plan going forward and a division of responsibilities, and (3) discuss some alternatives to the two of us working in different locations for the most of the day. For example, could we agree to work together at the project site during certain hours to increase our work efficiency? Should I consider working from home some as well, so I don't build up unwarranted frustration, and have time to pick up my dry cleaning to boot? Most importantly, I would try to set expectations with my colleague regarding work style and shared workload expectations. At this point, I might also consider taking our agreed-upon work style plan to the project manager, and make sure that she doesn't have a preference one way or the other about us working at the project site or from home – after all, it is her client and her relationship.

The interviewee provided a good response to this question. She was careful not to jump to any conclusions about the situation. Just like in a business case, it's important to list all the possible reasons for an observed trend before you dive into analyzing what you believe to be the core issue. The interviewee asked a lot of questions to find out more information about the situation. Most importantly, she allowed for the possibility that, despite the frustration described in the case question, the colleague's performance is not actually problematic.

The interviewee also used humor judiciously in her response to this question, opening her response with a somewhat tongue-in-cheek reference to her eagerness to get the job. Much of the quality of an answer to a question like this one lies in the nuances of delivery – do you seem friendly, relaxed, appealing to work with? When our interviewee plays the role of asking about his colleague's work hours over a sandwich, he is careful not to sound passive-aggressive. He spends most of the case gathering information from the interviewer rather than jumping to conclusions, but makes sure to wrap up his answer with a decisive, clear plan of action.

Notice that the interviewer switched from playing the role of interviewer to actually playing the role of the colleague. Be prepared to engage your interviewer in a realistic role-playing exercise – your interviewer is likely very interested not only in your theoretical approach to the situation, but how well you can articulate and communicate these types of delicate interpersonal issues face-to-face.

Difficult Situation Case #2: Bad News

As a senior associate at Killer Consulting, you are working on a project with a more junior associate and a partner. At this moment, the partner is on a plane flying across the country to deliver the final presentation and recommendations to the client at a senior executive meeting this afternoon. You and the associate worked very long hours and late nights to produce the financial analysis, prepare an initial draft of the presentation for your partner, and then polish up the presentation with his edits. The final results showed that it was worth $500 million to the client to invest millions of dollars in capacity expansion, which was the outcome the client team lead had been hoping for. In fact, the partner had already e-mailed your client team lead that the analysis had shown good news, and had followed that e-mail up with a phone call.

You are enjoying your usual morning coffee when the junior associate rushes into your office. He says, "Bad news. I found a major error in the model. The results are all wrong. Actually, the best alternative is to scale back production significantly and lay off hundreds of employees."

What do you do?

You:	Wow. Did that really happen?
Interviewer:	Yes, it did. Scary, isn't it?
You:	All right, let me play back the situation to you, just to make sure I'm clear. (*Repeats above information.*) I'd like to take a few minutes to gather my thoughts.
Interviewer:	Sure. Take your time.
You:	Great. (*Approximately one minute goes by.*) Okay, I think the basic approach is to first understand the

situation, then escalate the issue honestly, first to the partner and then to the client. I have some questions.

Interviewer: Fire away.

You: I think the important thing here is to stay calm. There are two issues here. First, at this point, I don't know that the model indeed has a problem and I need to verify that it does. Second, I need to handle communication and logistics; for example, I need to make sure I can reach the partner so we can discuss the situation, and I need to figure out when and how we will update the final presentation if we have to.

Interviewer: That seems reasonable.

You: Let me start asking some questions about the first issue. How familiar am I with the model, and am I conversant enough in Excel such that I can walk through the model with the associate?

Interviewer: You have built similar models in this industry in the past, so you're pretty familiar. You have seen this particular model only once or twice, but you should be able to figure it out if the associate calmly walks you through the issue.

You: Good, so I know I can address the problem hands-on. I would also like to know some logistics information regarding my partner's flight. How reachable is he, relative to flight connections and the client presentation?

Interviewer: The partner is flying across the country. It's 8:30 a.m. now and you find out from his assistant that his first flight leg lands at 9:45 a.m. and his connection takes off at 10:30 a.m. He will land at 2:00 p.m. The client presentation is at 3:00pm.

You: Did his assistant say he had his cell phone with him?

Interviewer: Yes, he has his cell phone with him.

You: Then let's get moving. As I mentioned before, I think a key step is to get in touch with the partner. I would leave him a message on both his cell phone and his work voice mail and classify them as "urgent." I wouldn't say that there is definitely a problem. I would say exactly what has happened, that the associate has communicated to me the strong possibility that we have a bug in the model, and my next step is to rigorously work through the model with him and verify it. I would tell the partner that I was calling to alert him to the need to check in with us when he was in the airport awaiting his connecting flight, so it would be best if he called me at that point in the office.

Interviewer:	Interesting. But why even bother the partner if you don't know there's a problem for sure?
You:	If I don't set up the need to communicate with the partner ahead of time, by the time we figure out if the problem is there or not, it'll be too late and he'll be on the plane. As the senior associate, I should take the initiative to think ahead this way.
Interviewer:	Makes sense. Now what?
You:	Now we look into the problem. I sit down with the associate, and we go through the model. The associate is probably panicking at this point, and I need to help him. Before he goes right to the problem, he needs to take a few minutes to explain to me just enough about how the model works so I can ask the right questions. Then I can ask good questions about the bug he found.
Interviewer:	Let's say that about half an hour later, you are convinced that there is a problem and the associate is right. Now what?
You:	I was afraid of that. Now I need to think about how we communicate to the partner and have some ideas regarding how we communicate this to the client. There's the issue of how it happened, and there's the more important issue of what we do about it. Let me ask: has this been a particularly demanding project in terms of work schedule?
Interviewer:	Yes, but the client is probably only nominally aware of it.

Visit the Vault Consulting Career Channel at **www.vault.com/consulting** — with insider firm profiles, message boards, the Vault Consulting Job Board and more.

VAULT CAREER LIBRARY   181

You:	Here's what I say to the partner when he calls: we have been working very hard on this project, and unfortunately we have found a bug in the model that changes the results dramatically. I would explain the issues we found at a high level and give him just enough information to understand, and I would allow him to ask questions. Then I would suggest a forward plan. We should redo the full analysis while the partner is in the air, and we should reframe the client presentation today as a discussion of the results that would warrant a follow-up discussion. I'm not sure it makes sense to cancel the presentation – what would we tell them? I would leave it to the partner to have a one-on-one with the client team lead to give a heads-up on the results, then restructure the 3 p.m. meeting or think about postponing it entirely.
	While it's not totally clear to me if we could have the meeting or not, I think it's clear we need to be honest with the client. This is bad news for them, and we want to help them make the right decision. I also think we need to be honest that we made a mistake. Perhaps this final presentation has been scheduled too early. There are many possibilities that could surface, but it has to start with honesty.
Interviewer:	Do you think the associate needs to be reprimanded for having a bug in the model? Or fired, even?
You:	Well, it's not necessarily the associate's fault. Perhaps we had too much work to do, perhaps the partner didn't keep a close enough eye on us, perhaps I should have been more involved in the modeling. It's very unclear and ineffective to take anything other than a team-based approach. I would try very hard to maintain a "we" focus – we found a bug, we made a mistake, we think that we should be honest. Also, we have been working hard and mistakes happen. I think it would crucial, though to have a team feedback session on this to discuss how the problem occurred and how we can avoid it in the future. This needs to involve the partner, the associate, and me. I think we can frame the situation

positively in retrospect once we are out of the fire and really treat it as a learning situation.

Interviewer: Great answers. Let me throw in a wrinkle here and change the situation slightly. Suppose that instead of being in the office while the partner is on the plane to deliver the results of the analysis, you are on the plane because the partner is ill and cannot make the presentation. While waiting for your connecting flight, you check your cell phone messages and find that the associate has left you an urgent message stating that the model results are incorrect and to please call back right away. When you return the associate's call, you learn that the analysis shows that the best course is to scale back production. You know the client won't be at all happy about this, especially the layoffs. How does this change your answer?

You: Very interesting. I think I need a little more information. First of all, when is the client presentation in this situation, relative to my flight times?

Interviewer: Same as before, it's at 3:00 p.m. Assume the flight times are the same for you as they would have been for the partner.

You: So I have about 20 minutes to chat with the associate, and I have a few hours to myself on the plane. Also, do I have access to the final version of the model?

Interviewer: Yes, you have the model on your laptop computer, which you have with you.

You: Okay. I think my answers stay very similar but this is a much higher pressure situation. As before, I would try to contact the partner to put him on alert, even though he's ill. I sit with the associate and work for 20 minutes before my flight leaves to understand the problem, and hopefully that's enough time, though there's a chance it's not. After that I need to spend a few minutes with the associate talking about next steps and who's going to redo the final presentation slides, and I need to have a conversation with the partner, probably after I have boarded the plane, about what we found and how we're

Visit the Vault Consulting Career Channel at **www.vault.com/consulting** — with insider firm profiles, message boards, the Vault Consulting Job Board and more.

VAULT CAREER LIBRARY   **183**

going to deal with it. Then, I have a few hours to work on the plane to recreate my portion of the final presentation. When I land, I need to have a private chat with the client team lead to go over how we will address these changes. It would be helpful to conference in the partner as well for this conversation. Again, honesty is the right approach.

In summary, my reaction in this situation should be very similar to my reaction in the previous one. But because I'm in the driver's seat instead of my partner, I need to be even more action-oriented.

This is a tough question with no real right answer, and the candidate gives a solid effort. One reason is because she chooses to take her time to think through the situation and comes up with a basic framework (working the communication/logistics and core problem in parallel). Remember that it is always reasonable to take a few moments to collect and structure your thoughts.

As far as the content of the discussion, notice how the candidate seems to work calmly and focus on a solution-oriented frame throughout. She is highly proactive as well – for example, she calls the partner right away to communicate the issue, then she sits down with the associate and starts walking through the model to ensure the new results are valid.

This is also a good example of how heightening communication with the team works well. Beyond the use of the "urgent" classification function in voice mail, she stresses the importance of clarity about the state of things at each junction. In her first voice mail to the partner, she says that there might be a problem and focuses on making sure she could reach the partner when they knew more; in the absence of concrete information on the problem, the focus is on setting up the day for successful communication and execution.

Most important here is the integrity the senior associate showed. She remained honest and had no interest in hiding mistakes or covering up bad news. She also maintained a "we" focus without blaming the associate, and assumed responsibility. Finally, framing the incident in terms of future learning shows maturity and long-term firm thinking.

Difficult Situation Case #3: Double Duty

You are a new MBA at Austin Consulting Group, and you are currently working on two projects. You are supposed to allocate 50% of your time to each project. However, midway into each project you find yourself feeling completely overwhelmed. Supposedly, both partners know that you are on two projects, yet you feel like you are more like 75% allocated to each project. You have been working extremely hard, including all-nighters and weekends. What do you do?

This is a highly typical situation for new consultants – don't be surprised if you get this question, and don't be surprised if you find yourself dealing with this very issue in your first year on the job.

Start with a inquiry frame. Remember, this is your first job out of business school – perhaps it feels like you are working way too hard, but maybe this is really just how it is on the job and you are taking a while to adjust. You might want to ask some of the more junior consultants who have been at the firm a year out of business school about their experiences. If similar to yours, then you may have to chalk it up to adjustment period. If markedly different, then you know it's more about your situation. Perhaps you are working for two especially demanding partners and your situation is unique. Or, it could be your firm culture to work extremely hard, which might raise some long-term questions for you.

Consider timing when you think about what to do about it. If these are both short projects (four weeks) then you might just want to deal and give it your all for the next two weeks. On the other hand, if you are midway into two ten-week projects, then you probably need to address the situation. Wait until after the mid-project presentations or another similar milestone, then approach each partner.

You will want to focus on a few things in these conversations:

- Start with some feedback on the positive aspects of the project from your perspective.

- Give examples of how the work was overwhelming and added up to more than the allocated 50%. Try suggesting to the partner what 100% would look like and therefore showing that you did more than "half."

- Frame your concerns at two levels. At the project level, you are concerned that having too much work to do on this project will deteriorate your performance for this client. At the firm level, you are concerned about poor performance on both. If the partner pushes back and says you seem to be doing just fine, explain how that may be true from the outside, but you're very concerned about how much longer this could last.

- Give concrete suggestions on where you could scale back the work. The partner may react well but also might resist. In all likelihood you will need to negotiate a little bit.

- Suggest that you have weekly (or other appropriate) checkpoints to make sure things are going well from the partner's perspective.

- Thank the partner for his or her time and understanding, and reiterate your commitment to the project.

Difficult Situation Case #4: The Crazy Boss

You and another associate are working together on a project. Things are going really well – the client is very happy with your consulting firm's work. However, whenever your project supervisor shows up things seem to fall apart. Members of the client team have recently mentioned how much the project supervisor bugs them. He seems disorganized and often takes meetings off track with wild ideas. How would you handle this situation?

As with any case question, start by clarifying the situation and gathering more information: What is your personal relationship to the project manager? What is your reporting relationship to him? What is his personality, and is he known to take feedback well? How concerned were the clients really? Is their assessment of the project manager accurate? Are there any interpersonal or political issues that could be clouding people's perceptions in this situation?

Ultimately, you are going to have to initiate a conversation with the project manager. Two well-established principles of effective feedback may come into play here:

- Feedback should always be given at an appropriate time and within a safe space. Rather than approach your project manager in the heat of crunch week, wait for a natural break in the project work and suggest a mutual feedback session.

- Feedback should always be based on observed facts, and never be framed in a personal manner. "The client expressed concern to me…"

or "I've observed that…" is far superior to "You always…" or "It bothers me when…"

The complicating factor here is that the person who requires feedback from you is your direct supervisor on the project. You probably don't want to overreact by immediately going over the project manager's head to his supervisor. Generally, consulting firms look for independent problem-solvers to execute client work, and would expect that same trait to carry over into interpersonal working relationships as well. Thus, your first reaction should not be to tell the project manager's supervisor, but instead to try speaking directly with the project manager to solve the problem. People have different perspectives on the same situation – what seems like a problem to you may not in fact be "wrong" behavior.

Nonetheless, you should take care to express serious concern for the client's comments about this issue. Consulting is all about client service. If the initial conversation with the project manager doesn't resolve things to your satisfaction, you would be obliged to also speak with the relevant partner. After all, the partner is always ultimately responsible for that client's business with your firm.

Difficult Situation Case #5: Formatting Wars

You and another new associate are both working on a strategy project that involves creating a large PowerPoint deck. For the past several days, you have both been adding slides into the deck – which is stored on the office LAN – that summarize pieces of analysis you have both done. Each time the file goes from one person's control to the others, the two of you make some formatting changes as well. The problem is that you are both changing the same format elements back and forth from one person's preferred style to the other's: numbers inside tables go from having a "k" abbreviation for thousand to showing extra zeroes; footnotes go from 10pt to 12pt and back again; gridlines appear and disappear from graphs… It is getting very aggravating. What do you do?

This is a very common issue, and an example of where small changes can cause major headaches.

Start with better understanding the situation and the division of responsibilities that the two of you have been assigned: is this person your exact peer? Are you two alerting each other about the changes, and rationales for them? Was one of you responsible for the analytics and other responsible for the PowerPoint development? Does your firm have formatting standards such that there is actually a "right answer" on which format is correct? How important is this deliverable – an informal interim report, a final project summary?

Most consulting firms have established some form of formatting standards for PowerPoint slides, which probably includes a master slide template that all employees are asked to use. Much of a consulting firm's brand image to the clients is conveyed through the format, layout, and information density of its PowerPoint outputs. As a result, formatting is a non-trivial matter. In addition, principles of information design suggest best practices for PowerPoint design: convey the most information possible with the least "ink" possible, all information on a given slide should support the header statement. Depending on whether the presentation will be delivered in-person as a walk-through, or delivered as a stand-alone report for the client's review, standards about font sizes and amount of text per page vary.

However, there are certain formatting issues (such as the ones you and your colleague are battling over) that the firm may not have an official policy on. In this case, the most important issue is creating visual consistency throughout the presentation so that it forms a cohesive whole.

The right thing to do is to work out this situation directly with your peer – going to the project manager first reveals a lack of problem-solving initiative on your part. Find a calm and safe time to bring up the issue with your colleague, and explain with fact-based arguments why it's important to agree on a common formatting practice for this presentation. You can suggest to the interviewer that an efficient solution to this situation is to assign one person to be responsible for formatting and one for content Q&A.

If you cannot easily come to an agreement with your colleague, approaching the project manager is a fine suggestion, provided you frame it correctly. You are not asking your project manager to intervene in an interpersonal situation. Rather, you are asking for her seasoned opinion on which format standards are most appropriate for this presentation and this client. You would explain to the project manager that your concern is creating a visually consistent, easily legible presentation that reflects well on your firm, so you want some guidance for the team as to which way you should go on certain issues.

Additional Practice Questions – Difficult Situations

1. You are the business analyst working on a client project with a project manager and a partner. The client team consists of a client team lead and a client manager. You are finding that the client manager continues to ask

you individually for additional analysis and information. In an effort to make the client happy, you have always complied and even stayed up late into the night to pull to this together. Your partner and project manager are unaware of this. The ongoing feedback from the client team lead is that your team is "going the extra mile" and she is looking forward to more of the same. You are exhausted from several consecutive nights of doing the incremental work for the client and fear this is finally cutting into your performance on your other work, but you also don't want the client to see performance scaled back. How do you handle this situation?

2. At DEF Partners, you are a lateral hire from ABC Consulting, a firm known for its internal efficiency in running projects for clients smoothly. At your first project meeting at DEF, which is being run by a senior partner in your office, you are shocked to see that there is no meeting agenda, no formal project timeline, no one is taking discussion notes, and the senior partner isn't documenting action items that people are signing up for. The next meeting reveals more of the same scattershot approach, with the addition that some of the team members didn't do their action items. Subsequent meetings are very similar. You feel that this firm is wasting time by being so inefficient and you are getting very frustrated, yet on the last conference call you heard the client describe how pleased he was with DEF's progress. How do you handle this situation?

3. You are an MBA-level consultant managing a third-year undergraduate analyst on a project. The project consists of Excel spreadsheets and a Powerpoint presentation. Typically, the more senior consultant (you) will structure and put together the presentation while the analyst crunches the numbers. On several occasions, the analyst has asserted that he would like to work on the presentation piece, for his own career development. You know that you both have more than enough work to do, and each time you explain to the analyst that you don't think the analyst could juggle both the presentation and the Excel modeling. This morning, you get an urgent voice mail from your partner on the project saying to stop by her office, because the analyst "shared with her some concerns about you holding back his career development on this project." How should you handle your subsequent conversations with both the partner and the analyst?

Consulting Interviews by Phone

As times change, so does the way consulting firms hire. Another trend worth discussing is how to handle interviews over the phone. If you're not interviewing as part of an annual campus recruiting cycle, you will in all likelihood be dealing with this. The first step is typically a phone screen with a recruiter, followed by the case interview over the phone.

Phone screening by HR

Having a recruiter conduct an initial phone screen of candidates seems to be a relatively recent phenomenon (i.e. over the last few years) in the consultant interviewing process. The primary reason for this step seems to be volume handling. Consulting jobs have been relatively scarce over the last few years, and the numbers of resumes that hit the recruiter's inbox for each new position that is advertised has swelled by an order of magnitude. Consulting senior manager and partners don't have time to interview all of the qualified candidates, so they rely on HR (and occasionally junior consultants) to conduct phone screens. Phone screens are primarily about your background and why you are seeking this position, so you will rarely have a case interview question come up.

You can prepare for the phone screen by thinking through the highly concise, incisive version of your story. Keep in mind that the next step in the process is for the recruiter conducting the phone screen to pass along notes to a partner for evaluation; what do you want those notes to say? What you say should be crystallized into a form that the recruiter can capture and communicate well, so be ready with the show answer as to why you should be considered. (Hint: you can write this out ahead of time. After all, you are on the phone and the recruiter can't see you.)

Case interviews by phone

The basic interview format for a phone interview is the same: fit questions, case question, and questions for your interviewer. The bad news, as some of us by now have realized, is that it's incredibly difficult to make the same impression over the phone that you could in person. Ever try to tell a joke to someone over the phone and get greeted by silence? Sometimes people need to see your face to know what you really mean – or, as in the case with phone interviews, you simply need to tell them more explicitly.

Here's another thing: have you ever noticed that your in-person interviewer may not be able to see exactly what you're writing on your page, but they can see and are therefore aided by the layout of what you're writing? This helps you in your in-person interviewer because you are providing the interviewer with mental guidance. For example, they can see you jotting down those bullet points for your case structure; when you indent, they are mentally indenting as well and know that what you're saying (or where your pen is pointing) refers to the "outer" bucket. When you outdent, they know you're going to talk about the next major point. In other words, the visual aid of watching you take notes helps them follow your framework better. (Interesting, huh?) Over the phone, you don't get the benefit of this guidance.

Keep in the mind the following tips for doing case interviews by phone.

- Describe your case structure in detail. Suppose your main topics were market size, competition, and products, with two or three bullet points beneath each main topic. You might explain your structure as follows: "There are three topics I'd like to address: market size, competition, and products. Under market size, I'd like to discuss X and Y. Under competition, I'd like to discuss Z. So, to recap, market size, competition, and products seem to be the key areas to focus on." You are essentially telling your interviewer how to replicate your structure over the phone; that is the level of detail you will likely need in order for the interviewer to follow your thinking.

- Be very straightforward with communication. Try to avoid highly nuanced comments that would be more effective in person. Good-natured sarcasm might work face-to-face but not in a phone interview.

- Overexplain your calculations. To be safe, you need to be extremely explicit about what you're calculating. Here is an example: "I'm going to shift to calculation mode for a second. I want thirty percent of 800 people, which is 240 people. So we'll use 240 people as our market size." This is probably one level of detail greater than you might have in person.

- Prepare your interviewer for pauses in the action. What if you need to take a few seconds to ponder a question? Say so. "That's a good question. Let me take ten seconds to process that." In person, you would prep your interviewer for your thinking time but you might not need to set the light expectation of how long he has to wait.

GUESSTIMATES

"Guesstimate" Case Interviews

Guesstimate questions are among the most unnerving questions you may ever have to answer in an interview situation. They can be so "off the wall" as to shake up an otherwise calm, collected candidate.

The approach to guesstimates is basically the same as business cases – you will showcase your ability to analyze a situation and form conclusions about this situation by thinking out loud. The difference here is that you will not necessarily be using a series of questions to gather feedback from the interviewer. Instead, you will drive toward a conclusion through a series of increasingly specific analyses. Let's look at an example:

> **How many ping-pong balls fit in a 747?**

This is an actual question used in consulting interviews. If you are a little unsettled by this type of question, it's no wonder. That is exactly the reaction the interviewer is expecting. Remember that the main objective of these questions is to evaluate your poise and professionalism when facing an outlandish situation. How you react to this question when presented will speak volumes about your ability to be professional when faced with a similar business situation at a client.

So, how do you approach a guesstimate question? First, don't panic. If you are visibly shaken when presented with a guesstimate or brainteaser, it will hurt you. It is extremely important that you do not lose your cool.

Do not let yourself struggle verbally. You are free to say something like, "That is an intriguing question. May I have a moment to think it through?" This statement immediately shows the interviewer you are still in control and gives you some breathing time to think about a method for answering.

Once you have had a minute to compose your thoughts, be sure and go through your reasoning out loud, so your interviewer can see that you're arriving at your answer in a logical manner. "Don't be anal," suggests one former consultant. "You should realize that for the purposes of a guesstimate, 1,000,553 is the same as a million, and you can divide by 350 if you need to divide by the number of days in the year."

Finally, remember that there is no right answer for guesstimates. It will often not even be necessary to come up with a definitive response like "1,400,350," due to constraints on time. Always work toward a final answer, but do not feel that you have done a poor job if the interviewer moves on to other topics before you are finished. They may simply recognize that you're on the right track and see no reason to keep going.

Acing Guesstimates

The best approach for a guesstimate or brainteaser question is to think of a funnel. You begin by thinking broadly, then slowly drill down towards the answer. Let's look at this approach in context. Referring to our sample question, you know that you are looking for how many ping-pong balls fit in a 747 airplane. The first thing you need to determine is the volume of the ping-pong ball.

For any guesstimate or brainteaser question you will need to understand whether your interviewer will be providing any direction or whether you will have to make assumptions. Therefore, begin the analysis of a guesstimate or brainteaser question with a question to your interviewer, such as, "What is the volume of a single ping pong ball?" If the interviewer does not know or refuses to provide any answer, then you will know that you must assume the answer. If the interviewer does provide the information, then your approach will be a series of questions. For this example let's assume your interviewer wants you to make the assumptions. Your verbal dialogue might go something like this:

Let's assume that the volume of a ping-pong ball is three cubic inches. Now let's assume that all the seats in the plane are removed. We'll say the average person is six feet high, one foot wide and one foot deep. That's 6 cubic feet, or 10,368 cubic inches. (One cubic foot is 12x12x12 inches, or 1,728 cubic inches.)

Okay, so a 747 has about 400 seats in it, excluding the galleys, lavatories, and aisles on the lower deck and about 25 seats on the upper deck. Let's assume there are three galleys, 14 lavatories, and three aisles (two on the lower deck and one on the upper deck), and that the space occupied by the galleys is a six-person equivalent, by the lavatories is a two-person equivalent, and the aisles is a 50-person equivalent on the lower deck and a 20-person equivalent on the upper deck. That's an additional 18, 28, and 120 person-volumes for the remaining space. We won't include the cockpit since someone has to fly the plane. So there are about 600 person-equivalents available. (You would be rounding a bit to make your life easier, since the actual number is 591 person equivalents.)

In addition to the human volume, we have to take into account all the cargo and extra space – the belly holds, the overhead luggage compartments, and the space over the passengers' head. Let's assume the plane holds four times the amount of extra space as it does people, so that would mean extra space is 2,400 person-equivalents in volume. (Obviously, this assumption is the most important factor in this guesstimate. Remember that it's not important that this assumption be correct, just that you know the assumption should be made.)

Therefore, in total we have 3,000 (or 600 + 2,400) person-equivalents in volume available. Three thousand x 10,368 cubic inches means we have 31,104,000 cubic inches of space available. At three cubic inches per ball, a 747 could hold 10,368,000 balls. However, spheres do not fit perfectly together. Eliminate a certain percentage – spheres cover only about 70 percent of a cube when packed – and cut your answer to 7,257,600 balls.

You might be wondering how you would calculate all these numbers in your head! No one expects you to be a human calculator, so you should be writing down these numbers as you develop them. Then you can do the math on paper, in front of the interviewer, which will further demonstrate your analytical abilities.

You choose the numbers, so pick nice round numbers that are easy for you to manipulate. Even if you just read a study that states that there are 295 million inhabitants in the United States, no interviewer will flinch if you estimate the number of American inhabitants as 300 million.

Quick guesstimate numbers

You'll need to grab numbers for guesstimates quickly. Here are some basic stats.

There are approximately 295 million people in the United States (but you can round up to 300 million for the purposes of guesstimates). By comparison, there are 1.2 billion people in China.

• There are about 100 million households in the United States.

• There are over 90 million people online in the United States.

• Approximately 50 percent of all Web users are English speakers.

• Forrester Research estimates that by 2004, $6.8 trillion will be spent on e-commerce online.

There are approximately eight million people in New York City, 13 million people in Shanghai, 3.5 million people in Los Angeles and seven million in London, England.

The extra step

Don't forget to add the "extra step" into your guesstimate. If you're trying to figure out how many blocks there are in New York City, remember to eliminate blocks covered by Central Park (and other parks). If you're determining the number of black cars in the United States, once you've estimated the number of cars in America, make sure you estimate what percentage of them are black.

In-case guesstimates

Not all guesstimates are stand-alone questions. Many are contained within case questions, mostly in the form of a market sizing. (And what would you say is the size of the market for pork rinds in the United States?) The key here is to derive a reasonable (and easily manipulated) figure for your calculations.

Practice Guesstimate Questions

The following are examples of guesstimates and suggested solutions. There is more variation here than in business cases. Whereas in business cases we ask that you make no assumptions, here you may have to make assumptions if your interviewer does not provide any additional information.

Remember to ask your interviewer each time you begin a guesstimate answer if they will provide information or if you will need to make assumptions. If you do, be sure to be perfectly clear where and when you are making assumptions.

This set of questions can be presented as either assumptive or with feedback from the interviewer.

1. How many gallons of white house paint are sold in the U.S. every year?

The "start big" approach: If you're not sure where to begin, start with the basic assumption that there are 270 million people in the U.S. (or 25 million businesses, depending on the question). If there are 270 million people in the United States, perhaps half of them live in houses (or 135 million people). The average family size is about three people, so there would be 45 million houses in the United States. Let's add another 10 percent to that for second houses and houses used for other purposes besides residential. So there are about 50 million houses.

If houses are painted every 10 years, on average (notice how we deftly make that number easy to work with), then there are 5 million houses painted every year. Assuming that one gallon of paint covers 100 square feet of wall and that the average house has 2,000 square feet of wall to cover, then each house needs 20 gallons of paint. So 100 million gallons of paint are sold per year (5 million houses x 20 gallons). (Note: If you want to be fancy, you can ask your interviewer whether you should include inner walls as well!) If 80 percent of all houses are white, then 80 million gallons of white house paint are sold each year. (Don't forget that last step!)

The "start small" approach: You could also start small, and take a town of 27,000 (about 1/10,000 of the population). If you use the same assumption that half the town lives in houses in groups of three, then there are 4,500 houses, plus another 10 percent, then there are really 5,000 houses to worry about. Painted every 10 years, 500 houses are being painted in any given year. If each house has 2,000 square feet of wall and each gallon of paint covers 100 square feet, then each house needs 20 gallons – and so 10,000 gallons of house paint are sold each year in your typical town. Perhaps 8,000 of those are white. Multiply by 10,000 – you have 80 million gallons.

Your interviewer may then ask you how you would actually get that number, on the job, if necessary. Use your creativity – contacting major paint producers would be smart, putting in a call to HUD's statistics arm could help, or even conducting a small sample of the second calculation in a few representative towns is possible.

2. What is the size of the market for disposable diapers in China?

Here's a good example of a market sizing. First, you might estimate that there are one billion people living in China. Because the population of China is young, a full 600 million of those inhabitants might be of child-bearing age. Half are women, so there are about 300 million Chinese women of childbearing age. Now, the average family size in China is restricted, so it might be 1.5 children, on average, per family. Let's say two-thirds of Chinese women have children. That means that there are about 300 million children in China. How many of those kids are under the age of two? About a tenth, or 30 million. So there are at least 30 million possible consumers of disposable diapers.

To summarize:

	1 billion people
x	60% childbearing age
=	600,000,000 people
x	1/2 are women
=	300,000,000 women of childbearing age
x	2/3 have children
=	200,000,000 women with children
x	1.5 children each
=	300,000,000 children
x	1/10 under age 2
=	30 million children

3. How many square feet of pizza are eaten in the United States each month?

Take your figure of 300 million people in America. How many people eat pizza? Let's say 200 million. Now let's say the average pizza-eating person eats pizza twice a month, and eats two slices at a time. That's four slices a month. If the average slice of pizza is perhaps six inches at the base and 10 inches long, then the slice is 30 square inches of pizza. So four pizza slices would be 120 square inches. Therefore, there are a billion square feet of pizza eaten every month.

To summarize:

There are 300 million people in America.

Perhaps 200 million eat pizza.

The average slice of pizza is six inches at the base and 10 inches long = 30 square inches (height x half the base).

The average American eats four slices of pizza a month.

Four pieces x 30 square inches = 120 square inches (one square foot is 144 inches), so let's assume one square foot per person.

Your total: 200 million square feet a month.

4. How many pay phones are there on the island of Manhattan?

There are two ways to handle this problem. First of all, you could estimate how many blocks there are in Manhattan, and assume that 75 percent of all blocks have a pay phone. (Remember, the interviewer didn't say they had to work.) If there are about 15 avenues across Manhattan, and if the island is 300 streets long, then there are about 4,500 intersections. If every intersection indicates a block, then there are 4,500 blocks in the city. That means 3,000 pay phones. Now add the extra step and subtract the size of Central Park. Say that Central Park is 50 streets by six avenues – that means you lose 300 blocks, or 200 pay phones. You have the figure of 2,800 pay phones. Now estimate how many pay phones exist in bars, restaurants, schools, etc. There may be a total of 3,500 pay phones in Manhattan. (This question is also sometimes used with estimating the number of manhole covers in Manhattan.)

5. How many weddings are performed each day in Japan?

Try a ground-up approach. In a city of 1 million (Kyoto), how many people are of marriageable age? Let's say 750,000. How many get married in a given year? Maybe 2 percent? That's 15,000. Now, the population of Japan is about 150 million, so multiply 15,000 by 150 – and you get 2.25 million weddings every year. Divide that by 365 and you get 6,164 weddings per day (on the average, though clearly some days are more popular than others).

To summarize:

There are 1 million people in Kyoto.

750,000 are of marriageable age.

2 percent get married in the average year.

750,000 x 0.02 = 15,000 marriages every year in Kyoto.

There are 150 million people in Japan.

150 x 15,000 = 2.25 million weddings per year.

2,250,000/365 = 6,164 weddings per day.

6. How many children are born every day in the United States?

The population of the United States is 300 million (approximately). Half are women (150 million). Perhaps half of those are of childbearing age. How do you determine how many women are pregnant at any given time? Well:

Let's say the average span of childbearing for a woman is 40 years.

The average woman has two children.

So a woman is pregnant one year in 20, or 5 percent of the time.

3.75 million women are pregnant every year.

Divide by 365 – you get about 10,000 babies a day (actually, 10,273).

Do the extra step – round up for multiple births, so perhaps 12,000.

7. How much change would you find on the floor of an average mall?

This seemingly silly guesstimate was received by a job seeker at McKinsey. It's an example of a guesstimate that is also a way to test candidate's "out-of-the-box" thinking. First, estimate how many stores there are in the average mall – say, 50. Now, how many people enter the average store on the average day? A thousand? So if there are 50,000 visitors to a mall daily, how many lose change? If one in 50, say, drops money (1,000 people a day), how much is the average loss of change? Most amounts are probably small. People carry fewer quarters, for example, and are more likely to retrieve them. So let's say that if a person is equally likely to drop a penny, nickel, or dime, then the average person who loses change loses a nickel. That means there would be $500 worth of change on the average floor. If half of that change has been picked up immediately, that would be $250 worth of change.

Also ask: Is there a fountain in the mall? If a fountain is considered to be the "floor" of the mall, the amount of change would obviously increase.

8. How many bottles of wine are consumed in the United States each week?

Determine:

1. The number of people in the United States.

2. The number of adults.

3. The number of wine drinkers.

4. Average number of glasses of wine consumed per week.

5. Number of glasses of wine in an average bottle.

(Extra step: You may wish to estimate how much wine is used for non-drinking purposes – cooking, for example. Also clarify whether the interviewer is speaking of standard-sized bottles of wine.)

You could reasonably make the following assumptions:

There are about 300 million people in the United States.

250 million are adults.

Perhaps 220 million drink alcohol.

200 million drink wine.

The average wine drinker drinks two glasses of wine a week.

400 million glasses of wine consumers per week.

About five glasses of wine in the average bottle.

80 million bottles of wine consumed in America each week.

Estimate how many bottles of wine are used for cooking – perhaps another five million.

This brings your total to 85 million bottles of wine consumed per week.

More Guesstimates...

9. How many men's suits were sold in the United States last year?

Determine:

1. Estimate the population of the United States.

2. Cut that in half to get the number of men.

3. Determine how many men are employed in occupations which require business attire.

4. Determine how many suits the average business attire employee would have purchased (due to weather, fashion changes, cleanings, wear, and so on).

5. Assume (or ask) a number of suits that those men not employed in business attire jobs purchased for religious, social, or other reasons.

6. Sum up the number and present your answer.

To summarize:

The population of the United States: 270 million (or 300 million, to round up).

Half are men – so 150 million.

Let's say two-thirds are employed.

150 million x 2/3 = 100 million.

Assume every employed man owns one suit = 100 million suits.

Estimate that about a quarter of men are in a field where they must own more than one suit.

If each of those men has an additional two suits, 25 million men x 2 additional suits = 50 million suits.

150 million suits in the United States.

How often does the average suit-owner replace a suit? Perhaps once every three years.

There are 50 million suits sold every year in the United States.

10. How many tennis balls fit in a swimming pool?

Determine:

1. What is the shape and depth of the swimming pool?

2. What is the volume of a tennis ball?

3. Estimate the volume of the swimming pool based on the depth, length, and width of the pool.

4. Calculate the number of balls by dividing the volume of the pool by the volume of the tennis ball.

5. You may wish to subtract balls due to steps in the pool and the gradual upslope of the pool due to the varying depth (but ask first).

11. How many gas stations are there in Los Angeles?

Determine:

1. What is the population of Los Angeles?

2. What is the number of cars in Los Angeles? What is the average number of cars per person (including commuters)?

3. How many gas stations are needed per car?

12. What is the annual size of the golf ball market in the United States? What factors drive demand?

Determine:

1. What is the population of the United States?

2. What percentage of the population golfs?

3. How often does the average golfer golf?

4. What is the number of balls used in an average golf game (and number that are lost)?

What factors drive demand?

- How many golf courses are being built in the United States?

- How many are planned?

- Is the population of golfers (due to Tiger Woods and his ilk) expanding?

13. Estimate the total revenues of Disney's Tarzan.

Here's where some prior knowledge comes in handy.

Determine:

1. What were movie ticket revenues in the United States for *Tarzan*?

2. What percentage of worldwide sales is the U.S. revenue?

3. How much does Disney make from video sales?

4. What are Disney's revenues from cross licensing agreements (dolls, posters, etc.)?

And Try These for More Practice...

14. How many red cars are there in the United States?

15. What is the annual demand for table napkins in the United States?

16. How many times would the population of China circle the globe if they held hands?

17. What is the size of the poultry market in the United States?

18. How many people are cremated in the United States every year?

19. How many barbers are there in New Orleans?

20. What is the annual market for peaches in the United States?

21. What are the revenues of the Plaza Hotel in New York City?

22. How many hotel-size bottles of shampoo and conditioner are produced each year around the world?

BRAINTEASERS

Brainteasers

You might be taken aback when your interviewer suddenly asks you: "So, if you were selling a television and your neighbor was selling the identical set for half the price, what would you do?" Or, perhaps, that beloved (by interviewers) chestnut "Why is a manhole round?" Some of these questions have no set answer. Instead, the interviewer is assessing creativity, composure, your ability to deconstruct the problem, and finally your ability to ask directed and relevant questions. Others do have answers, which you are expected to reason out calmly, quickly and logically. "Cases and guesstimates are given to candidates to test reasoning skills, but be warned – brainteasers are sometimes given to test your poise under stress," says one consultant.

Remember...

Brainteasers are very unstructured, so it is difficult to suggest a step-by-step methodology. There is one set rule, though: Take notes as your interviewer gives you your brainteaser, especially if it's mathematical in nature. Other than that, you may select any starting point you are comfortable with and then ask directed questions around the answers you get back from the interviewer. You may need to break the question down into several parts depending on its complexity, but it is not important to start in any particular place.

Every year consulting firms tell us they discourage the use of brainteasers – and every year we hear about candidates getting them.

Practice Brainteasers

1. Why are manhole covers round?

The classic brainteaser, straight to you via Microsoft (the originator). Even though this question has been around for years, interviewees still encounter it. Here's how to "solve" this brainteaser. Remember to speak and reason out loud while solving this brainteaser!

Why are manhole covers round? Could there be a structural reason? Why aren't manhole covers square? It would make it harder to fit with a cover. You'd have to rotate it exactly the right way. So many manhole covers are round because they don't need to be rotated. There are no corners to deal with. Also, a round manhole cover won't fall into a hole because it was rotated the wrong way, so it's safer.

Looking at this, it seems corners are a problem. You can't cut yourself on a round manhole cover. And because it's round, it can be more easily transported. One person can roll it.

2. The power has gone out in your hotel room, and it is pitch black. You have 11 white socks and 10 black socks in your suitcase. (It's a long-term engagement.) You must put on a matched pair of socks, or you'll look terrible at your presentation! How many socks must you pull from the drawer to be assured of a matched pair?

Don't be fooled! Either white or black will do, so you need only three socks to be sure of either a white or black matched pair.

3. You are in a room with three light switches. Each controls one of three light bulbs in the next room. You must determine which switch controls which bulb. All lights are off. You may flick only two switches and enter the room with the light bulbs only once. How would you determine which switch controls which light bulb?

This is an invitation from the consulting firm to express your "out-of-the-box" thought patterns. Staring in disbelief, whimpering in fear, or otherwise reacting negatively will shoot down your chances. So be creative. Ask if you can pull out your cell phone and call a pal for assistance. Run out and buy a drill so you can peek through the wall. There is, however, one especially elegant solution. Turn one light bulb on for about twenty minutes. Then turn it off. Turn another switch on. Then enter the room and feel the two bulbs that are off. The hot one will be attached to the switch that you just turned off. Using all your senses – that's thinking like a consultant!

4. You are in a rowboat on a lake with the anchor dropped. You pull up your anchor. Does the water level in the lake rise, lower, or stay the same?

The intuitive answer for many is to say that the water level remains the same – but it doesn't. It rises, becasue the anchor displaces a larger volume of water when it is pulled up and in the boat than when it is on the bottom of the lake.

5. You have 12 balls. All of them are identical except one, which is either heavier or lighter than the rest. The odd ball is either hollow while the rest are solid, or solid while the rest are hollow. You have a scale, and are permitted three weighings. Can you identify the odd ball and determine whether it is hollow or solid?

This is a pretty complex question, and there are actually multiple solutions. First, we'll examine what thought processes an interviewer is looking for, and then we'll discuss one solution. (This question is reportedly in use at McKinsey, incidentally.)

Start with the simplest of observations. The number of balls you weigh against each other must be equal. Yeah, it's obvious, but why? Because if you weigh, say three balls against five, you are not receiving any information. In a problem like this, you are trying to receive as much information as possible with each weighing.

For example, one of the first mistakes people make when examining this problem is that they believe the first weighing should involve all of the balls (six against six). This weighing involves all of the balls, but what type of information does this give you? It actually gives you no new information. You already know that one of the sides will be heavier than the other, and by weighing six against six, you will simply confirm this knowledge. Still, you want to gain information about as many balls as possible (so weighing one against one is obviously not a good idea). Thus, the best first weighing is four against four.

Secondly, if you think through this problem long enough, you will realize how precious the information gained from a weighing is: You need to transfer virtually every piece of information you have gained from one weighing to the next. Say you weigh four against four, and the scale balances. Lucky you! Now you know that the odd ball is one of the unweighed four. But don't give into the impulse to simply work with those balls. In this weighing, you've also learned that the eight balls on the scale are normal. Try to use this information.

Finally, remember that consultants love out-of-the-box thinking. Most people who work through this problem consider only weighing a number of balls against each other, and then taking another set and weighing them, etc. This won't do. There are a number of other types of moves you can make – you can rotate the balls from one scale to another, you can switch the balls, etc.

Let's look at one solution:

For simplicity's sake, we will refer to one side of the scale as Side A and the other as Side B.

Step 1: Weigh four balls against four others.

Case A: If, on the first weighing, the balls balance
If the balls on our first weighing balance, we know the odd ball is one of those not weighed, but we don't know whether it is heavy or light. How can we gain this information easily? We can weigh them against the balls we know to be normal. So:

Step 2 (for Case A): Put three of the unweighed balls on Side A; put three balls that are known to be normal on Side B.

I. If on this second weighing, the scale balances again, we know that the final unweighed ball, is the odd one.

Step 3a: Weigh the final unweighed ball (the odd one) against one of the normal balls. With this weighing, we determine whether the odd ball is heavy or light.

II. If on this second weighing, the scale tips to Side A, we know that the odd ball is heavy. (If it tips to Side B, we know the odd ball is light, but let's proceed with the assumption that the odd ball is heavy.) We also know that the odd ball is one of the group of three on Side A.

Step 3b: Weigh one of the balls from the group of three against another one. If the scale balances, the ball from the group of three that was unweighed is the odd ball and is heavy. If the scale tilts, we can identify the odd ball, because we know it is heavier than the other. (If the scale had tipped to Side B, we would use the same logical process, using the knowledge that the odd ball is light.)

Case B: If the balls do not balance on the first weighing

If the balls do not balance on the first weighing, we know that the odd ball is one of the eight balls that was weighed. We also know that the group of four unweighed balls are normal, and that one of the sides, let's say Side A, is heavier than the other (although we don't know whether the odd ball is heavy or light).

Step 2 (for Case B): Take three balls from the unweighed group and use them to replace three balls on Side A (the heavy side). Take the three balls from Side A and use them to replace three balls on Side B (which are removed from the scale).

   I. If the scale balances, we know that one of the balls removed from the scale was the odd one. In this case, we know that the ball is also light. We can proceed with the third weighing as described in Step 3b from Case A.

   II. If the scale tilts to the other side, so that Side B is now the heavy side, we know that one of the three balls moved from Side A to Side B is the odd ball and that it is heavy. We proceed with the third weighing as described in Step 3b in Case A.

   III. If the scale remains the same, we know that one of the two balls on the scale that was not shifted in our second weighing is the odd ball. We also know that the unmoved ball from Side A is heavier than the unmoved ball on Side B (though we don't know whether the odd ball is heavy or light).

Step 3: Weigh the ball from Side A against a normal ball. If the scale balances, the ball from Side B is the odd one, and is light. If the scale does not balance, the ball from Side A is the odd one, and is heavy.

Whew! As you can see from this solution, one of the keys to this problem is understanding that information can be gained about balls even if they are not being weighed. For example, if we know that one of the balls of two groups that are being weighed is the odd ball, we know that the unweighed balls are normal. Once this is known, we realize that breaking the balls up into smaller and smaller groups of three (usually eventually down to three balls) is a good strategy – and an ultimately successful one.

Visit the Vault Consulting Career Channel at www.vault.com/consulting — with
insider firm profiles, message boards, the Vault Consulting Job Board and more.

VAULT CAREER LIBRARY   **215**

6. You are a king, with a hundred princes and princesses in your kingdom. Every year, the princes and princesses must bring you a bag of one hundred gold coins that weigh one ounce each. But you have learned there is a traitor in your realm. He or she will bring you hollowed out coins this year – and then strike at you! You are allowed to do one traditional weighing of coins on a scale. How will you use this opportunity to flush out the traitor?

Various versions of this puzzle have been making the rounds on the brainteaser circuit. Here's how to tame this problem (and to reason its solution out loud). First of all, if you ask if you can mark a coin from each prince and princess, your interviewer will tell you no – that would be far too easy! You'll need to find another way to solve this dilemma. The key is that you must find a way to somehow "mark" which prince or princess donates which coin. Number each prince and princess from one to 100. Then tell each to put that number of coins onto the scale. Calculate how much the group of coins should weigh, and determine how many ounces you're short. That number of ounces is also the number of the traitor. Guards!

7. You have a five-gallon jug and a three-gallon jug. You must obtain exactly four gallons of water. How will you do it?

"They gave this question even after *Die Hard with a Vengeance* came out!" says one outraged consultant. But whether you've seen that gimmicky, puzzle-based movie or not, you should find this brainteaser pretty simple. Fill the three-gallon jug with water and pour it into the five-gallon jug. Repeat. Because you can only put two more gallons into the five-gallon jug, one gallon will be left over in the three-gallon jug. Empty out the five-gallon jug and pour in the one gallon. Now just fill the three-gallon jug again and pour it into the five-gallon jug. Ta-da.

8. You are faced with two doors. One door leads to your interview (that's the one you want!) and the other leads to the exit. In front of each door is a consultant. One consultant is from a firm that always tells the truth. The other is from a firm that always lies. You can ask one question to decide which door is the correct one. What will you ask?

Clearly, you can't just ask a consultant which is the correct way – one of them will lie to you. The important thing is to work in a double negative. Ask a consultant: "If I were to ask you if this door was the correct one, what would you say?" The truthful consultant will, of course, answer yes (if it's the correct one) or no (if it's not). Now take the lying consultant. If you asked the liar if the correct door is the right way, the liar will answer no. But if you ask the liar how they would answer if you asked them the same question, the liar will be forced to lie about the fact that they would say no – and answer yes.

Another solution is to ask a consultant: "If I were to ask the other guy which way to go, what would he say?" The reasoning is similar – except in this case, you should go the opposite way.

9. You have 100 black marbles and 100 white marbles. You have two jars into which to place the marbles. You must randomly select a marble, and you wish to maximize your odds of choosing a black marble. How do you distribute the marbles, and what are your odds of choosing a black marble after you make your distribution?

If you place all the black marbles in one jar and all the white marbles in another, your chances will be 50/50. Your best bet is to put one black marble in one jar and all the other marbles in the other one. In the one jar, the chance of picking the black marble will be 100 percent. In the other one, your chance is 49.5 percent. Averaged, your chance of grabbing a black marble is 74.75 percent.

How many consulting job boards have you visited lately?

(Thought so.)

Use the Internet's most targeted job search tools for consulting professionals.

Vault Consulting Job Board

The most comprehensive and convenient job board for consulting professionals. Target your search by area of consulting, function, and experience level, and find the job openings that you want. No surfing required.

VaultMatch Resume Database

Vault takes match-making to the next level: post your resume and customize your search by area of consulting, experience and more. We'll match job listings with your interests and criteria and e-mail them directly to your inbox.

FINAL
ANALYSIS

Final Analysis

Case questions can be very disturbing if you haven't encountered them before. You may have prepared well for the standard interview questions like "Tell me about yourself," and "Describe your greatest achievement." But case questions stretch your poise, professionalism, analytical abilities, and deductive reasoning power in ways in which consultants are asked to perform every day. If you become comfortable with this line of questioning by practicing and preparing, you will be well equipped to meet the difficulty of these questions. Try to have fun with the challenge of the case interview. The more you enjoy solving problems and using your analytic and creative ability, the better you'll do and the more fun you'll have. Good luck – practice, don't be nervous (all interviewers were candidates once), and crush those case interviews!

APPENDIX

Consulting Glossary

Consultants often lapse into their own lingo while conversing with civilians, thus further panicking those who were unaware that they possessed something called a "skill set" (for what it's worth, the things that you're good at). Following is a basic list that can raise your level of familiarity with consulting terms that consultants like to fling about in case interviews:

Bananagram: A graph showing profitability (the typical measure of profitability for this graph is return on capital employed, or "ROCE" [pronounced roachy]) vs. relative market share. The graph shows that the higher the market share, the higher the profitability.

BCG matrix: A portfolio assessment tool developed by BCG. Also called a growth/share matrix.

Benchmarking: Measuring a value or practice or other business measure (such as costs) against other companies in the industry.

Blank slide: Initial sketch on paper for a slide to be used in a consulting case presentation (called blank because it does not include data until analysts put it in).

Brainteaser: A type of consulting interview question in which the job seeker is asked to solve a logic problem.

Business Process Re-engineering (BPR): BPR is the process of reviewing a client's business processes, eliminating unneeded or "non-value-added" tasks, and then implementing the leaner, more efficient process.

Case team: Team that works on a consulting project for a client. Usually composed of one partner (or director), one consultant, and two or more analysts.

Change management: One of the services provided by consulting firms, in which the firm helps a company cope with a period of significant change (such as a merger, downsizing or restructuring).

Consultancy: A typically European name for what we call a "consulting firm" in the U.S., though the term has picked up currency in the U.S.

Convergence: The trend toward industries uniting. (For example, cable TV customers may someday be able to place telephone calls using cable technology, while telephone customers may be able to receive television through phone lines.)

Core competencies: The areas in which a company excels. Consultants believe a company should enter only those businesses which are part of its core competencies.

Critical path: This term comes from Operations Management theory. Every business process is made up of a series of tasks. Some of these tasks are related to maintenance of the process or administrative and bookkeeping issues. Taken away, they do not directly impact the end result of the business process. If you eliminate these non-meaningful tasks, you are left with the core set of tasks that must occur in order for the process to produce the desired result. This is the critical path. In everyday consulting language, it is used to refer to only those work tasks which are the most important at the time.

Customer Relationship Management (CRM): Term that refers to the data-gathering methods used to collect information about a client's customers. Usually focuses on sales force automation, customer service/call center, field service, and marketing automation.

DCF: (Discounted Cash Flow). The present value of a future cash flow.

Drilldown: Asking questions to gather more detail about a situation, usually from a high-level (big picture) view.

80/20 rule: Getting 80 percent of the answer first will take 20 percent of your time. The other 20 percent of your time may not be worth it.

Engagement: A consulting assignment received by a consulting firm. Also called a "case" or "project."

Enterprise Resource Planning (ERP): Processes or software that help streamline departments or divisions of a company.

Experience curve: The principle that a company's costs decline as its production increases. One assumption used by consultants is that a company's costs decline by roughly 25 percent for every doubling in production (e.g. a company's 200th unit of a product costs 75 percent of the 100th unit's cost).

Granularity: This simply refers to the basic elements that make up a business problem. Imagine a handful of sand. At a high level it's simply a handful of sand; at a granular level it is bits of many different kinds of rock and shell matter reduced to fine granules over time by the action of the ocean. Consultants are not usually this poetic.

Guesstimate: A type of consulting interview question. Guesstimates require job seekers to make an educated estimate of something (often the size of the market for a particular product or service) using basic calculations.

Helicoptering: See High-level view.

High-level view: This is also referred to as a "50,000-foot view." It refers to describing a situation in general terms or as an overview.

Hoteling: Consultants move around so much that in some firms they are not assigned permanent offices, just a voice mail extension. Each week, they must call up the office nearest them to request a desk. This is called "hoteling."

Hurdle rate: A company's cost of capital. In general, if the return on an investment exceeds this "hurdle rate," the company should make the investment; otherwise, the company should not.

Implementation: The process by which a consulting firm ensures that the advice it gives to a client company is enacted.

Learning curve: The rate at which a consultant acquires background information or industry knowledge needed for a case. A "steep" curve is a good thing.

NPV: (Net present value). The sum of a series of discounted cash flows. Used to assess the profitability for a client of making an investment or undertaking a project.

O'Hare test: A test consultants use in interviews to assess personality "fit." If I was stuck overnight with this person at O'Hare airport, would I have fun?

On the beach: For consultants, the spare time between assignments, when their work hours decline drastically. Consultants between assignments are said to be "on the beach" (not literally). This expression originated at McKinsey.

Out-of-the-box thinking: Creativity.

Outsourcing: Taking a process normally performed within a company and hiring an outside vendor to perform the task, often at a lower cost and with better results. Examples of processes that are commonly outsourced include: payroll, data processing, recruitment and document processing. Outsourcing is a growing trend among corporations.

Reengineering: A largely discredited fad of the early 1990s, which advocates a complete overhaul (and usually downsizing) of a company's strategies, operations, and practices.

Rightsize: Also "downsize," this is just a kinder, friendlier term for restructuring the elements of a company. This is most often used in reference to headcount reductions, but can apply to plants, processes, technology, financial elements, and office locations.

Shareholder value: The wealth of a company's stockholders or their equity (ownership) in the company. The primary goal of consultants in undertaking any engagement is to increase shareholder value.

Stakeholder: A critical person who has a stake in the outcome of a particular situation. Most commonly, the stakeholders in a case are the shareholders, creditors or employees.

Total Quality Management: Also known as TQM. Management with the purpose or intent of producing a product or offering a service of the highest quality, with zero tolerance for defects.

Value migration: The flow of economic and shareholder value away from obsolete business models to new, more effective designs.

Value-added: Used to define a service or product in a marketplace that adds value to a pre-existing product or way of doing things.

Workplan: A schedule for completing a consulting engagement.

Writing a deck: Preparing slides for presentations to clients.

White space opportunity: An opportunity for a company to make money in an area in which they are currently generating zero revenue (for example, launching a new product line, licensing an existing brand or technology, or entering a new geographic market).

Visit the Vault Consulting Career Channel at **www.vault.com/consulting** — with
insider firm profiles, message boards, the Vault Consulting Job Board and more.

VAULT CAREER LIBRARY   **229**

About the Authors

Mark Asher: Mark is a consultant with PricewaterhouseCoopers.

Eric Chung: Having spent his childhood as a quant jock and later as a theoretical physics major in college, Eric is now applying his analytical skills to a career in consulting. Eric spent three years at Goldman Sachs, where he developed proprietary accounting and financial management systems for the firm. During business school, Eric was active in the management consulting group and was selected to teach a full-quarter class on leadership and communication skills to first-year students.

After spending a summer during business school interning at Accenture, he is currently a consultant with Strategic Decisions Group, a boutique firm specializing in decision making under uncertainty. He is also an active violinist, singer, songwriter, and director of a cappella singing groups. Eric is a graduate of Harvard College and the University of Chicago Graduate School of Business.

Are you trying to get into the consulting job market or trying to move to another firm? The job market is tough – and you need every advantage you can get.

How many consulting job boards have you visited lately?

(Thought so.)

Use the Internet's most targeted job search tools for consulting professionals.

Vault Consulting Job Board

The most comprehensive and convenient job board for consulting professionals. Target your search by area of consulting, function, and experience level, and find the job openings that you want. No surfing required.

VaultMatch Resume Database

Vault takes match-making to the next level: post your resume and customize your search by area of consulting, experience and more. We'll match job listings with your interests and criteria and e-mail them directly to your inbox.